I0192782

Nicolls' Outpost

A War of 1812 Fort at Chattahoochee, Florida

Dale Cox

2015

Copyright 2015 by Dale Cox
All Rights Reserved

ISBN: 978-0692379363

Old Kitchen Books
4523 Oak Grove Road
Bascom, Florida 32423

And they shall go into the holes of the rocks,
and into the caves of the earth, for fear of the LORD,
and for the glory of his majesty, when he ariseth
to shake terribly the earth.
Isaiah 2:19

Contents

Introduction

During the final year of the War of 1812, British forces built two forts on Florida's Apalachicola River. One of these, the British post at Prospect Bluff, is well known today and the site is preserved at Fort Gadsden Historic Site in the Apalachicola National Forest. The second is seldom mentioned by modern writers, although it was the stronghold from which Great Britain planned to launch its actual conquest of the State of Georgia. It stood atop a prehistoric Indian mound at Chattahoochee Landing on the east bank of the upper Apalachicola.

The British did not follow the American custom of naming their wartime forts and camps, so their establishments on the Apalachicola River were known by them simply as the "British Post" and the "British Fort." The former was the establishment at Prospect Bluff 18 miles above Apalachicola Bay that American forces later called the "Negro Fort" and Fort Gadsden. The latter was dubbed "Nicolls' Outpost" by historian Mark F. Boyd in the 1950s and the name remains in use today.

This is the story of Nicolls' Outpost and its role during the closing days of the War of 1812. It is a story of military confrontations, a clash of empires and of the desperate stand by Red Stick Creek warriors and African American colonial marines to preserve their freedom and way of life.

The writing of this volume would not have been possible without the help and encouragement of numerous individuals and repositories. Special appreciation is due the staffs of the National Archives and Library of Congress; the Florida, Georgia and Alabama State Archives; the Georgia Historical Society; Willard Library in Evansville, Indiana; W.C. Bradley Library in Columbus, Georgia; the State Library of Florida in Tallahassee; Dr. Brian

Rucker of Pensacola State College; Dr. Nancy White and Erin McKendry of the University of South Florida; Roger Moore and Douglas Mangum of Moore Archaeological Consulting, Inc.; Brian Mabelitini of Gray & Pape, Inc., Sue Tindel, archivist for Jackson County, Florida; Gregg Harding of the University of West Florida; Dr. Dean DeBolt, Stephanie Johnson and Brooke Bowers of the University Archives & West Florida History Center of the University of West Florida.

Special thanks also are extended to the wonderful people of Chattahoochee Main Street and the City of Chattahoochee for their interest in preserving, interpreting, and enhancing the site of Nicolls' Outpost at River Landing Park. Great things are in the future for Chattahoochee because its residents care about the future of their community and are working together to give the city new life. Thank you also to the West Gadsden Historical Society for helping with the new historical marker seen on the cover. River Landing Park in Chattahoochee will become a major destination for heritage and eco-tourists entirely thanks to the interest of so many civic minded people.

Finally, I am grateful as always to my sons, William and Alan, and my mother, Pearl Cox, for suffering through my numerous historical discussions while I think out loud as I work on writing projects. My sincere appreciation must go to my editor, Savannah Brininstool, for her role in keeping my writing clear and on point. Than you also to Whitney Willis for taking the photo of me that was used on the back cover.

Finally, thank you to all of my friends, correspondents and readers for your encouragement, kindness and friendship. May God bless you with happiness and success.

Dale Cox
February 8, 2015

Nicolls' Outpost

A War of 1812 Fort at Chattahoochee, Florida

ONE

The arrival of the British on Florida's Apalachicola River in 1814 was presaged by a dramatic and violent upheaval in the Creek Nation of Alabama and Georgia. Josiah Francis, a wealthy and artistic mestizo living in the Alabama towns, had a revelation that he should both convert to and preach the religion of the Shawnee prophet. His message that the Creeks should abandon the ways of the whites, unite with other tribes to prevent any more land cessions, and return to their traditional ways had massive impact in a nation that had lost its way. Francis became a Hillis Hajod or "Maker of Mad Medicine," a title that testified to the power of his message and medicine.

The new Creek prophet led his followers to a bluff on the Alabama River where they established Ecunchatta or "Holy Ground." It was a town where the curious could come to hear the messages of Josiah Francis and learn more about the new religion that was sweeping the nation. From a small congregation of fewer than 100 in the winter of 1812-1813, his following grew to include thousands by the following summer.

The rise of the Prophet Francis was resented and feared by the Big Warrior, Little Prince and other traditional chiefs of the nation. They appealed to U.S. Agent for Indian Affairs Benjamin Hawkins for arms, troops and help. Hawkins, however, underestimated the power of the prophet and the strength of his following. When the traditional chiefs executed several of Francis' followers for their involvement in an attack on white families in Tennessee, a civil war erupted in the nation. To the shock of Hawkins and other whites on the frontier, the prophet's army drove the Big Warrior from his capital at Tuckabatchee and forced him to flee with his followers to Coweta on the Chattahoochee River. The Red Sticks, as Francis' followers were known, threatened to seize control of the entire Creek Nation.

As the war accelerated a party of warriors led by Peter McQueen of Tallassee went down to Spanish Pensacola to secure a resupply of ammunition and lead. As he was leading a train of horses laden with these supplies back to the Red Stick towns, McQueen was attacked at Burnt Corn Creek in Alabama by five companies of territorial militia. The outnumbered Red Sticks won the battle, a victory that was interpreted by the Creeks as a sign of the power of Josiah Francis and his movement. The bloody Red Stick attack on Fort Mims followed, an assault that ended with the deaths of hundreds of white and mestizo men, women and children.

Rumors of the upheaval reached the British in the Bahamas. The War of 1812 was then underway and Governor Charles Cameron in New Providence saw the potential for opening a new southern front against the United States. He sent Lieutenant Edward Handfeld in the HMS *Herald* to Pensacola with orders to learn what he could about the condition and attitudes of the Creeks and report back.

Handfeld reached the Florida city in September 1813, shortly after the Red Stick destruction of Fort Mims. There he encountered a party of chiefs from the Apalachicola and lower Chattahoochee Rivers. Uninvolved in the war, these leaders were terrified that it would spill over to their towns. They penned a letter to Governor Cameron and requested that Handfeld deliver it on their behalf:

We hope you will eade and assist us as your alis and friends Sir you know that our four fathers owned the Lan Where we now live But and Ever since our father the King of Grate Briton Left us the Americans had Ben Robing us of our Rights and now the americans has maid war against our nations and we aply for armes and amenisun to defend our silves from so Greid a Enemy and as you Know that this nations all ways was frinds to the English we hope you will send us Seplys by Henry Durgen as soon as possible and we hope that you will send sum of our old frind the British troops to eade and assist us a ganst our Enemeys.[1]

The leaders of the delegation that met with Handfeld were Thomas Perryman and his son William. Wealthy and powerful, they were the descendants of an English trader named Theophilus Perryman and his Eufaula Creek wife. Thomas had been designated a colonel and William a captain by the British during the American Revolution. Each led warriors in the fight against the American Patriots in Georgia. They also were close associates of the adventurer and pirate William Augustus Bowles during his two sojourns in

2

Florida. Bowles married a daughter of Thomas Perryman, thereby making himself the son-in-law of the old chief and the brother-in-law of William Perryman.

The nominal leader of the Creek towns on the Apalachicola and lower Chattahoochee and Flint Rivers, Thomas Perryman wanted to protect his followers against a spread of the war or American reprisals that might not distinguish towns that remained neutral during the Creek War from those involved in the Red Stick movement. He needed arms and ammunition from the British and he was desperate to get them. Lieutenant Handfeld carried the letter back to New Providence, taking along the interpreter Henry Durgen to better explain the situation to Governor Cameron. He reached the Bahamas on October 28, 1813.[2]

Sensing an opportunity, the governor moved quickly and dispatched a letter for England on the same day. In it he informed powerful Earl Bathurst of the situation in the Creek Nation and the pleas of the Perrymans and their allies for arms and ammunition. Bathurst replied on January 21, 1814, that he was authorizing the Royal Navy to supply the Creeks.[3]

Overall command of the operation fell to Vice Admiral Sir Alexander Cochrane. A fighting officer, he had led British flights in battle on numerous occasions. Perhaps the most remarkable moment of his career came in 1806 when took part in the Battle of San Domingo against Napoleon's French navy. His outgunned warship HMS.*Northumberland* was engaged in severe combat with a stronger French vessel when a cannonball passed so close to the top of his head that it carried away his hat. He was knighted as a Knight Grand Cross of the Order of the Bath, a level third only to the King and the Great Master. Both Houses of Parliament passed a vote of thanks in his honor. He was also presented with a sword and granted Freedom of the City of London. The latter honor gave him the right to lead military parades through the city.[4]

To carry out the orders of the Secretary of State for War and Colonies, Admiral Cochrane ordered Captain Hugh Pigot to deliver the arms and ammunition requested by the chiefs to the mouth of the Apalachicola River on Florida's Gulf Coast. Pigot was the commander of a small squadron consisting of the 36-gun frigate HMS *Orpheus* and the one-time American 12-gun schooner HMS *Shelburne*. Sailing south down the Atlantic Coast from their previous stations, the ships reached the Bahamas in the spring of 1814. Governor Cameron provided Pigot with considerable information on the Florida coast and introduced him to George Woodbine, a Bahamian trader, and Henry Durgen, the interpreter sent by the chiefs to represent them in New Providence.

Woodbine had spent time trading in Florida and seemed a logical choice to establish a beachhead at Apalachicola Bay. Neither Cameron nor Pigot seems to have been aware that he was a wanted man in Great Britain:

> *Whereas, at the Assizes, and General Session of Oyer and Terminer, holden at the Castle of Exeter, in and for the country of Devon, on Saturday, the 18th July, 1812, a Bill of Indictment for PERJURY, committed in a certain proceeding, instituted in the High Court of Admiralty, touching the employment of a certain ship or vessel, called the GALLICIA, in the Slave Trade, was at the instance of the Directors of the Africa Institution, preferred, and found against George Woodbine, otherwise called JORGE MADRESILVA, who acted as Super Cargo on board the said ship or vessel at the time of her capture, by His Majesty's ship Amelia, off the coast of Africa, in the year 1811; and the said George Woodbine, otherwise Jorge Madresilva, not having appeared to the same Indictment, he hath since been Out-lawed by due course of law. Notice is therefore, hereby given, that whoever shall apprehend the said George Woodbine, otherwise called Jorge Madresilva, and cause him to be lodged in the Castle of Exeter, or any other of His Majesty's Gaols in England, shall receive a REWARD of ONE HUNDRED GUINEAS from the Directors of the said Institution.[5]*

Circulated 1813 guineas were selling at between $825 and $4,125 when this volume went to print. The 100 gold guinea reward for Woodbine's arrest would be worth $82,500-$412,500 today.[6]

Pigot set sail for Florida with the holds of the *Orpheus* and *Shelburne* filled with arms, ammunition and other supplies for the Indians. Woodbine and Durgen both went with him aboard the *Orpheus* and were witnesses to the anti-climactic battle between British ships and the American warship USS *Frolic*. sail for Florida. The encounter took place on the morning of April 20, 1814, as Pigot's vessels entered the Florida Straits. The Americans did not uphold the best traditions of the U.S. Navy. The *Orpheus* had fired only two shots, both of which fell short, when the *Frolic* suddenly struck her colors. As the surprised officers and men of the Royal Navy approached to take possession of the 22-gun U.S. ship, they could see her sailors tossing their small arms and ammunition into the sea. A prize crew sailed the *Frolic* to New Providence while the *Orpheus* and *Shelburne* continued on to the mouth of the Apalachicola River.

Fifteen days later, as the ships made their way up the Gulf of Mexico, Pigot appointed Woodbine to the rank of 2nd lieutenant in the Royal Marines:

I do hereby constitute, and appoint you, to act as second Lieutenant of Royal Marines, on board His Majesty's Ship Orpheus. You are therefore carefully and diligently to discharge the duty of Acting Second Lieutenant of Royal Marines by exercising, as well as disciplining, both the Inferior Officers, and Marines belonging to the said ship, and I do hereby command them to obey you as their second lieutenant, and you are to follow such orders, and directions from your Captain or any of your Superior Officers....[7]

In addition to arming the Creeks and Seminoles, Woodbine would be tasked with helping to organize a battalion of Royal Colonial Marines. The troops and noncommissioned officers of this force would be men of color and the former slave trader would now command liberated slaves and free blacks in battle.

The *Orpheus* and *Shelburne* arrived off Apalachicola Bay on May 10, 1814. Neither Pigot nor Lieutenant David Hope of the *Shelburne* had a competent pilot to take them through West Pass and neither was willing to risk grounding on the shallows and oyster bars for which the bay is known. Both ships dropped anchor off the pass and displayed full colors to attract the attention of any Creek and Seminole warriors that might be in the area. Lieutenant Woodbine received his first promotion on the same day:

By Hugh Pigot Esqr.
Captain H.M. Ship Orpheus & Senior Officer West Florida

Sir,

In order the more effectually to perform the important service you are charged with,

I do hereby constitute and appoint you to act as Brevet Captain of the Royal Marines, until the pleasure of of the Commander in Chief is known, and you are hereby authorised to take upon you the charge and command of Brevet Captain accordingly.

Given on board the Orpheus
The 10th May 1814 off the
River Appalachicola[8]

The river off which the British had anchored is one of the most beautiful in the South. Rising 112 miles to the north at the confluence of the Chattahoochee and Flint, the Apalachicola River drains a total land area of 19,500 square miles. Its biodiversity equals that of the Great Smoky Mountains with numerous rare plant and animal species to be found along its banks. Alum Bluff, near Bristol, is the largest exposed section of the earth's crust in Florida. Local legend holds that the bluff and its adjacent ravines were the site of the Garden of Eden and that the rare Florida Torreya tree was the "gopher wood" from which Noah built the ark.

The Creek and Seminole towns along the river were under the nominal leadership of Colonel Thomas Perryman and extended from today's Alabama border south to a point about 30 miles upstream from Apalachicola Bay. The Perryman towns themselves were on both banks of the Chattahoochee River arm of the Apalachicola about 15 miles above present-day Chattahoochee. Colonel Perryman's town, Tocktoethla, was on the east side of the river in what is now Seminole County, Georgia. His son William Perryman was the principal chief of Tellmochesses, a town on the Florida side of the Chattahoochee but set slightly back from the river on higher ground. To the north just below the Alabama line was Ekanachatte while to the south along the main river were the villages of Tomathli, Hyhappo, Ocheesee, Blunt's Town and Iola along with a number of smaller settlements. The village of Tutalosee Talofa ("Fowl Town") had recently relocated down the Flint River to a site near today's Bainbridge, Georgia.

These towns identified themselves as Creek on some occasions and Seminole on others, an indication that the formation of what would become the Seminole Nation was still in a state of flux at the time. They were strongly allied with powerful Miccosukee who lived on the lake of the same name near Tallahassee. The Miccosukee considered themselves to be an independent people and were led by the aging chief Cappachimico. Sometimes called Kenhajo by the whites, he had been an ally of William Augustus Bowles during earlier times. Far to the east on the Suwannee River was Boleck's Town, the village of the Alachua chief Boleck who had been driven from his home on the Alachua Prairie by Tennessee troops just one year before.

The total strength of these towns is difficult to estimate, but the British believed they could raise a force of 2,500 to 3,000 warriors in Florida exclusive of the men from Coweta and other villages higher up the Chattahoochee and Flint Rivers. The American Indian population of North Florida in 1814 spoke a myriad of languages. Hitchiti was the prominent dialect of the region, but the Muskogee language was also common. Smaller groups spoke Yuchi, Alabama and even Choctaw.

European settlers were not completely unheard of in the region. John Forbes & Company maintained a trading post at Prospect Bluff 15 miles up the Apalachicola from the Gulf. The store employees, Edmund Doyle and William Hambly, each owned plantations higher up the river at Spanish Bluff on the west bank and near present-day Bristol on the east bank. John Mealy had long lived at Ocheesee where his son Jack was now the principal chief, but appears to have died prior to the War of 1812. The Spanish maintained the fort at San Marcos de Apalache (St. Marks) and other European, creole and mestizo settlers lived in villages across the area.

Likely informed by interpreter Henry Durgen that the larger towns were upriver well above the bay, Captain Pigot ordered Woodbine to proceed up the Apalachicola River and make contact with the principal chiefs:

You are hereby directed to proceed up the river Appalachicola and endeavour by every means in your power to procure an interview with the Chiefs of the Creek Nation. You will inform them that the Orpheus Frigate has arrived on the coast with two thousand muskets, ammunition, &c. &c. for them, and ... and should cavalry be able to act inform me what arms and furniture they stand in need of. [9]

Sergeant Samuel Smith and Corporal James Denny from the Royal Marines detachment onboard the *Orpheus* volunteered to assist Woodbine in this mission and agreed to accompany him on his journey up the river. They were instructed by Pigot to begin training the warriors in small arms tactics as soon as practicable. Woodbine was given the brevet or field rank of captain to facilitate his command of these efforts.[10]

How far this mission proceeded upriver or whether it departed at all is not clear, but contact was established with Thomas Perryman and Cappachimico who were invited down to receive arms and meet with the British. They arrived at the bay on May 20, 1814, and went aboard the *Orpheus* on the next day. The chiefs agreed that the British could construct a storehouse on St. Vincent Island for the deposit of the arms and supplies from the ships. They also agreed to the proposal that Sergeant Smith and Corporal Denny begin training their warriors. Captain Pigot gave orders to this effect on the same day, authorizing Smith and Denny to begin cooperating with the Indians in attacks on American troops:

By Hugh Pigot Esqr. Captain
His Majesty's Ship Orpheus & Senior Officer West Florida

It being for the good of His Majesty's Service, I feel it my duty to accept the voluntary offer of your services to instruct the Creek Nations in the use of small arms & assist them against our common enemy the Americans.
For which, it is my positive directions you put yourselves under the command of Brevet Captain Woodbine of the Royal Marines, and follow such orders as he may give from time to time for the performance of this service.

Given under my hand on board
the said ship the 21st May 1814.[11]

Just across the bay from the modern city of Apalachicola, St. Vincent Island is now a national wildlife refuge. Undeveloped and unspoiled, the island is enchantingly beautiful with 4,566 acres of wetlands, 5,861 acres of coastal forest, 387 acres of sand dunes and 1,412 acres of coastal shrub. It is home to a variety of unique species including American alligators, bald eagles, indigo snakes, red wolves, loggerhead sea turtles, gopher tortoises, wood storks and others. The British found St. Vincent to be pristine and wild but not particularly hospitable or easy to reach. Although the planned storehouse was built and supplies were landed, Woodbine quickly turned his attention to the Forbes & Company trading post at Prospect Bluff which could be reached with greater ease by warriors coming down the Apalachicola.

Fifteen miles upstream from the bay on the east side of the river, Prospect Bluff was called *Loma de Buena Vista* or "Hill of Good View" by the Spanish.

The bluff was not the commanding height that some modern writers have described, its surface being only 10 feet or so above the normal water level of the Apalachicola. It was, however, the lowest point on the river to which foot travel was possible throughout the year. Miles of swamps and wetlands surrounded it in all directions.

While virtually all of the modern scholarship about the War of 1812 on the Apalachicola River has focused on this low rise, it was not the primary objective of the British in 1814. Captain Woodbine's first report of his activities makes clear that the objective all along was the establishment of a post at the head of the river from which attacks could be launched against the State of Georgia:

...The Proclamation of the Commander in Chief, I intend to forward in a day or two to Georgia, Tennessee & New Orleans by trusty Indians, who have been appointed at a general meeting of the chiefs, for such purposes, and I have no doubt of several hundred American slaves joining our standard the moment it is raised, which shall be done when the arms are all up, and an encampment formed on the Forks of the River.[12]

The proclamation mentioned by the captain was an invitation for the Indians, white citizens and slaves of the backcountry to rise up against the United States and offer their loyalties to King George. If they did so, the document promised, they would be assured the protection of their rights and properties by British troops.

The "encampment" at the forks proposed by Woodbine would eventually be constructed and is the focus of this study. Events would intervene, however, to delay the planned project until the fall.

---

[1]Col. Thomas Perryman, Capt. Willam Perryman, Alexander Durant and Noah Hoeo to Governor of Providence, September 11, 1813, PRO CO 23/60.
[2] Lt. Edward Handfeld to Gov. Charles Cameron, October 28, 1813; Gov. Charles Cameron to Earl Bathurst, October 28, 1813, both from PRO CO 23/60.
[3] *Ibid.*; Earl Bathurst to Gov. Charles Cameron, January 21, 1814, PRO CO 24/14.
[4] Stephen Howarth, "Cochrane, Sir Alexander Inglis (1758-1832), *Oxford Dictionary of National Biography*, Index Number 101005749, online edition, September 2011.

[5] *London Times*, April 25, 1815.

[6] Conversion based on listed prices of 1813 gold guineas on December 28, 2013.

[7] Hugh Pigot to George Woodbine, May 5, 1814, Cochrane Papers (Signed aboard HMS Orpheus)

[8] Hugh Pigot to George Woodbine, May 10, 1814, Cochrane Papers (Signed aboard HMS Orpheus off the Apalachicola River).

[9] Hugh Pigot to George Woodbine, May 10, 1814, Cochrane Papers (Signed aboard HMS Orpheus off the Apalachicola River).

[10] *Ibid.*

[11] Hugh Pigot to Sgt. Smith & Corp. Denny, May 21, 1814, Cochrane Papers (Signed aboard HMS Orpheus off the Apalachicola River).

[12] Capt. George Woodbine to Capt. Hugh Pigot, May 25, 1814, Cochrane Papers.

Lt. Gen. Sir Edward Nicolls

Admiral Sir Alexander Cochrane

Capt. Robert C. Spencer, Royal Navy

Prophet Josiah Francis (Self-Portrait)
©Trustees of the British Museum.

Col. Benjamin Hawkins, U.S. Agent for Indian Affairs

Andrew Jackson (Late in Life)
Matthew Brady photograph courtesy Library of Congress

Nicolls' Outpost: A War of 1812 Fort at Chattahoochee, Florida

St. Vincent Island off Apalachicola, Florida

Apalachicola Bay in Florida

17

Julee's Cottage, home of a free woman of color in Pensacola.

LaValle House in Pensacola, has stood since before the War of 1812.

Nicolls' Outpost: A War of 1812 Fort at Chattahoochee, Florida

Apalachicola River at Prospect Bluff

Site of British Fort at Prospect Bluff

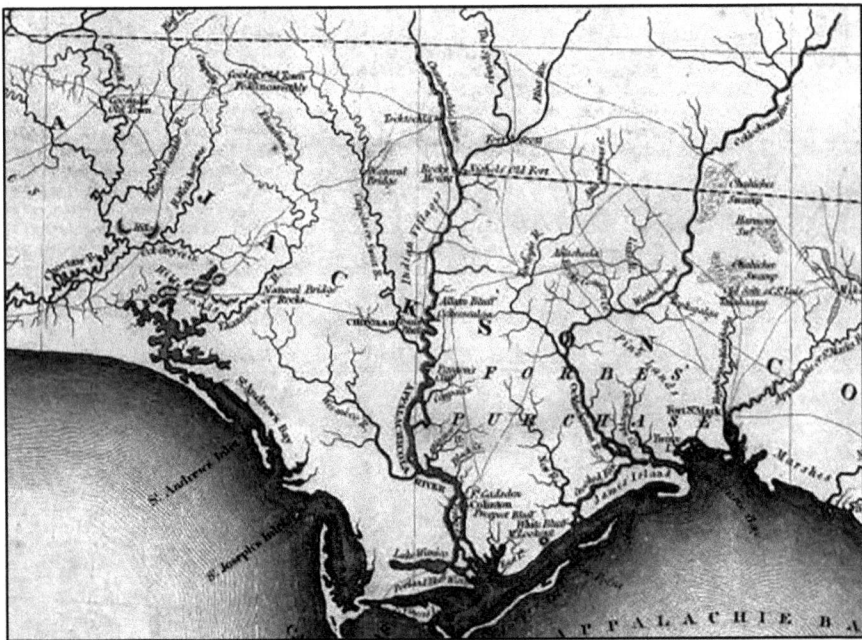

Apalachicola River, from Vignoles' Map of 1823
Courtesy of the Library of Congress

TWO

A Flood of Refugees

Captain George Woodbine reached Prospect Bluff on May 25, 1815. Using the John Forbes & Company store as a temporary headquarters, he convened a council with a small group of Creek and Seminole chiefs and warriors. Among the leaders represented were Thomas Perryman, Cappachimico and John Yellowhair. The latter individual was a sub-chief of Tomathli. Woodbine urged them to spread word through the towns and villages of the region that chefs and warriors were welcome to come to the bluff for arms and ammunition. It was not his intent at this stage of the campaign to remain there long, but instead saw Prospect Bluff as a supply depot to which materials of war could be moved from St. Vincent Island. As was noted at the end of the previous chapter, the captain's plan was to establish a fortified encampment at the head of the river to serve as his base of operations. St. Vincent Island and Prospect Bluff would remain important links in the supply chain that the British would have to use to get arms and ammunition up the river.

The council included a distribution of gifts to the chiefs and warriors present, followed by a talk in which Woodbine explained British strategy:

Your Father wishes to know what things you want to make you all happy. If you tell me, I will write to his Admiral and Great Warrior, who will send them. Your Father told me to tell you, that he wants to protect all the Indians and to make them into one family that they may unite and drive the Children of the Bad Spirit (the Americans) out of the lands and hunting ground. Your father told me to tell you that he wants some Americans, men women & children, and

*if you will take them all prisoners, instead of killing them, he will send you good
presents every year and plenty of Powder & Ball to hunt with.*
*You must bring them all to me his Captain, and I will write to the Admiral
and great Warrior, who will then write to the King your father, all good talks
about you.[1]*

After briefly considering the captain's offer as well as his request that the
lives of prisoners be spared, Cappachimico and the senior Perryman answered
with a positive response:

*In the name of all the chiefs of the Creek Nations, now assembled in arms
against the Americans, we promise to spare the lives of all prisoners taken,
wither man, woman or child, and to give them to Captain Woodbine of the Royal
Marines who has informed us that they should be a gratefull present to our
Father King George.*

For all the Chiefs, we sign by their desire,
Thomas Perryman, King of the Seminoles
Cappachamico, King of the Mickasukis

The two leaders placed their marks on a written copy of their agreement,
the signing of which was witnessed by Forbes employee William Hambly. He
would soon accept a commission as lieutenant in the Colonial Marines battalion
being raised by Woodbine.

The chiefs told the captain that they would be willing to fight for the British,
but only if Woodbine led them himself:

*At this same meeting the chiefs have unanimously decided that all power to
conduct operations shall be taken out of their hands and lodged solely in mine,
as chief of all, as also the appointment of all officers, and that no interference
of a single individual shall be allowed. This command I have accepted on
condition, that they will make prisoners (and give them up to me for the purpose
of working on any public works I may order) that they put to death no one but
those resisting with arms in their hands, which is agreed to, and all chiefs
individually have pledged themselves, that their tribes will comply. As the first
steps of authority I have nominated the two principal chiefs, old Perryman and
Cappichamicco Generals and joint with me to receive all reports and*

information and to consult upon all subjects; this measure appears to have given great satisfaction. They I know I can twist round my finger and induce them to think as I do, particularly the latter.[2]

Subsequent events would show that Cappachimico was not as twisted round Woodbine's finger as the captain believed. The chiefs likely felt considerable relief after learning that the British did not expect them to go to war on their own. They had no desire to see their warriors killed and towns destroyed by the soldiers of the United States. If the British were willing to land in force and Woodbine was willing to lead them, however, they were willing to fight.

Woodbine learned from the chiefs that the Red Sticks had suffered a devastating defeat at the hands of the U.S. army of Major General Andrew Jackson. The Battle of Horseshoe Bend had taken place on March 27, 1814, and had ended in the virtual annihilation of Menawa's army. More than 800 warriors died on the battlefield and as many as 200 more were thought to have been shot in the Tallapoosa River as they tried to escape by swimming away. Realizing that they could not hope to withstand a similar attack, Josiah Francis, Peter McQueen, Autossee Mico, Homathlemico and other Red Sticks led their bands of men, women and children south in a desperate flight to Spanish Florida. The chiefs informed Woodbine that thousands of these people were starving in the swamps of the Choctawhatchee, Yellow Water, Escambia and Conecuh Rivers.

John Yellowhair was sent as a courier to the refugee camps with an invitation for the displaced Creeks to come to Prospect Bluff for food, supplies and arms. The interpreter Henry Durgen, meanwhile, was sent to Pensacola to relay the same invitation to any Red Sticks that might be assembling there under the protection of the Spanish military. The British meanwhile focused on the construction of a large storehouse at Prospect Bluff. Despite the claims of some modern historians, no efforts were made to fortify the site at this time.

Captain Woodbine realized from his conversations with the chiefs that he would need large stocks of provisions to feed the desperate Creeks. Until massive shipments of food could be sent to the Apalachicola, he expected supplies would run short:

I am sadly afraid I shall be badly off for provisions up the country till the crops (which will be in six weeks at least) ripen. If I had two hundred barrels of flour to take up the river with me, I would carry destruction among the

Yankees, before three weeks. If you come across any vessel with provisions, I think you could most materially benefit the service by bringing him directly in. From some letters I intercepted yesterday from the American agent for purchasing cattle, the small body of troops they have in this nation are almost in a state of starvation, and the Indians with them are quite discontented on that account, so much so that I am offered their services by the Chiefs privately if I will victual them which I am at present unable to do.[3]

Woodbine reported that he had been joined by a small party of Choctaw warriors. They promised that their entire nation would join as soon as the British landed in force, a promise they would prove unable to keep.[4]

The British had been at Prospect Bluff only five days but the captain already had his sights set on attacking the American frontier:

The Admiral's proclamations are forwarded to Georgia, & Louisiana. I hope Sir Trowbridge will shortly arrive as you suppose and bring field pieces with him, had I had a gun in the launch I would have attacked Fort Mitchel about 200 miles up the river, both by water and land in less than 3 weeks. There is only one gun mounted on it and a garrison of 200 men. I however I don't despair having it and one or two more forts ere long.[5]

Fort Mitchell stood in what is now Russell County, Alabama, where it had been built in 1813 by the Georgia army of General John Floyd. It stood on the crest of a hill high above the Chattahoochee River and would have been more difficult to attack than Woodbine supposed, especially with William McIntosh and the U.S.-allied warriors of Coweta within supporting distance.

In a strange incident that could be interpreted as a supernatural warning of things to come, the captain reported that "lightning on Tuesday night struck a tree near the magazine and blew up one of the large casks of powder." One man was severely scorched in the incident. It would not be the last explosion at Prospect Bluff.[6]

American officials in Georgia learned of the British arrival on the Apalachicola with remarkable speed. The Big Warrior, Little Prince and mestizo trader John Stedham informed Agent Benjamin Hawkins of the Redcoat presence on June 13, 1814. A boat owned by Stedham had returned upriver from a trip to the John Forbes & Company trading post with electrifying news. A number of British officers and soldiers were at the store. The former asked for the use of Stedham's vessel to go to St. Vincent Island, but his boatmen refused and would not come to shore. The officers continued their entreaties until the crew finally complied and agreed to take them to the bay. When they reached the island they saw two warships off shore, one of which they described as a 50-gun ship while the other was smaller. The whole British force had landed on the island.[7]

The boatmen also reported that the British and their Indian allies had built four temporary storehouses on St. Vincent Island, one of which contained a massive stockpile of ammunition. Canoes and small boats were being used to carry supplies from the island up to Prospect Bluff. The two warships left the vicinity while Stedham's boat was still at St. Vincent Island and his employees reported that 50 British soldiers had been left behind. More troops were expected to arrive in 30 days.[8]

The report of Stedham's boatmen was remarkably accurate and gave Colonel Hawkins a clear picture of the actual situation on the lower Apalachicola. The British, he undoubtedly realized, were having serious logistical problems. They had not anticipated the need for small boats and were forced to beg, borrow or steal any vessel that might fit their needs. The shallow bar at the entrance to the bay forced them to move arms, ammunition and other supplies not just once but twice. Since the warships could not enter the bay, the British were forced to send everything first to the palm-thatched storage houses on the eastern end of St. Vincent Island and then from there up to the Bluff.

As the news of the British arrival struck the Georgia frontier with the impact of the lightning bolt that hit a powder keg at Prospect Bluff, a message suddenly arrived from Cappachimico who reported that he had attended a talk with the British but did not like their words. In what must have been either a ruse or an attempt to please both sides, he told the chiefs up the Chattahoochee that the British had offered him arms and ammunition but that he had refused. He said that the British officers called his warriors their children but that he remembered the talks of William Augustus Bowles in another time and would accept nothing from them but clothing, for which his people were suffering a shortage.[9]

There is no doubt that the Miccosukees had been taking arms and ammunition from the British, but it is definitely possible that Cappachimico had no plans of taking his people to war with the United States. He had long walked a delicate line in trying to maintain the neutrality and independence of his people. Continuing his talk, he indicated that he would cast his fate with the principal Lower Creek town of Cusseta and only go to war if Cusseta and Coweta agreed to do so first. A talk was to be held at Thomas Perryman's town, but it was being moved instead to Eufaula to allow for greater attendance. He promised to send the "broken days" so the chiefs would know when to come down.[10]

The announcement that a council would be held at Eufaula, a Creek town on the Chattahoochee River, is curious. According to Woodbine, Cappachimico and Thomas Perryman had already agreed to commit their people to fight alongside the British. The calling of this council, however, indicates that either the chiefs did not have the power that the British assumed or that they were simply telling Woodbine what he wanted to hear in exchange for arms, ammunition and supplies. The bloody defeat of the once powerful Red Sticks, hundreds of whom now lived as refugees in the Florida towns, could not have been lost on the old Miccosukee and Seminole chiefs.

Meanwhile, more information reached the Creek leaders about the activities of the British in Florida. They promptly relayed this to Colonel Hawkins, reporting that a warrior had been down to St. Vincent Island where he also saw two British ships. An officer told him that he had been sent to see whether or not the Indians had been destroyed in the Creek War and to offer them help. The man, probably Captain Woodbine, said he would give four casks of powder to each town that joined him, along with short muskets and other supplies. He claimed to have 1,000 soldiers in each of the ships.[11]

The report, attributed to the Wolf Warrior and "Fullausau Haujo" by Hawkins, went on to detail surprisingly accurate information about British plans for a coordinated attack from both Florida and the Georgia seaboard. The officer on the island urged the Upper Creeks or Red Sticks driven from their homes in Alabama to assemble between Pensacola and the Apalachicola River where they could be supplied. The British plan was to take Mobile, Perdido Bay, the mouths of the Yellow Water and Choctawhatchee Rivers, St. Mary's, an island

26

near Savannah followed by that city itself, and finally an island near Charleston.[12]

The British actually did have plans for such a campaign. Woodbine had sent Yellowhair to make contact with the Red Stick bands hiding along the Yellow Water and Choctawhatchee Rivers. The Royal Navy had plans to take Fort Bowyer at the entrance to Mobile Bay, the fall of which would open the way to the city of Mobile itself. The "island near St. Mary's" was Cumberland Island, which the British planned to occupy using a strike force under Rear Admiral George Cockburn, the same officer would give the orders to burn Washington, D.C., later that summer. That Woodbine knew so much about the planned Southern Campaign is surprising. Even more surprising is the fact that he discussed it so freely in his meetings with the Creek and Seminole chiefs at Prospect Bluff and St. Vincent Island. The Creek chiefs at Coweta and Cusseta immediately informed Colonel Hawkins of the growing threat.

Numbers of warriors from the Lower Creek towns headed down the Apalachicola to receive arms and ammunition from the British, although many had no plans to use them against the Americans. Some of these men brought back a report of a talk given at the Bluff by the Prophet Francis:

The Prophets observed to the Seminolies in the presence of the Reporters – "we have brought our difficulties on ourselves, without advice from any one – the old chiefs need not expect we will be given up. We have friends now, and if they attempt to follow us, we will spill their blood. We have lost our country and retreated to the sea side, where we will fight till we are all destroyed – we are collected, and find a few more than a thousand warriors left."[13]

Another Red Stick, Tustennuggee Hadjo, echoed the sentiments of the Prophet in a message he sent up the Chattahoochee to the Big Warrior of the Upper Creeks and Little Prince of the Lower. "I have now friends and arms," he stated, "you compelled me to fly and if you attempt to track me up I shall spill your blood."[14]

Benjamin Hawkins responded to these reports by urging the Creek chiefs to send out war parties to destroy the remaining Red Sticks, promising the support of the United States if they did so. He also reminded them of the misery brought on their Nation by the Prophet Francis and other followers of Tecumseh and his brother Tenskwatawa, the Shawnee Prophet. Tecumseh, he said, had told the Creeks during his famed speech in the square of Tuckabatchee to live in friendship and peace with all people and to do no harm to anyone of any color. His real meaning, Hawkins continued, had been much more sinister. The Shawnee leader intended for the Creeks to kill their traditional chiefs. All cattle, hogs and chickens in the Nation were to be destroyed, along with all signs of white culture to be found among them. If they did so, the ground would swallow any attacking American troops and the Red Sticks would be able to slay them with their war clubs. The colonel told the chiefs to go to the battlefields at Horseshoe Bend and Talladega to look at the fields whitened with the bones of Red Sticks if they wished to see the results of following the advice of the British, who he clearly believed were behind Tecumseh's efforts.[15]

Captain Woodbine, meanwhile, continued to face a serious supply shortage at Prospect Bluff. There were plenty of guns there, but very little food. As he did what he could to keep supplies moving, he ordered Sergeant Smith and Corporal Denny to proceed up the river to the forks of the Chattahoochee and Flint. Their presence there would prevent many warriors from coming on down to the bluff where they could not be fed. They would also serve as the advance in the planned effort to establish an encampment at or near the forks.

The two Royal Marines reached the confluence sometime in June, becoming the first British soldiers to enter American territory during the New Orleans campaign. Their primary mission was to begin training the hundreds of warriors that were concentrated in the towns near the forks. Most of these were now armed with muskets and bayonets provided by the British. While Smith and Denny trained the warriors in basic infantry tactics, they also spent time scouting possible locations for the construction of a fort. News of this did not take long to reach the trader Timothy Barnard who lived up the Flint River in Georgia.

Writing to a Mr. Munford on August 5, 1814, Barnard urged the citizens of the Georgia frontier to prepare for hostilities. A warrior from a town near his own had been down to the mouth of the Apalachicola River where he had seen 600 British soldiers, 300 of them black and the other 300 white. They planned to build a fort at Prospect Buff, he reported, followed by another at the junction of the Chattahoochee and Flint Rivers.[16]

Events were now unfolding rapidly in Georgia. No sooner had Barnard's report reached Milledgeville than did alarming news arrive of a raid by Creek warriors. The purpose of the incursion was to liberate slaves and carry them to the Apalachicola, where Captain Woodbine was seeking black recruits for a new battalion of Colonial Marines. Lieutenant Colonel Allen Tooke of the 35th Georgia Militia detailed the attack to Governor Peter Early on August 6, 1814:

> *It is with great pain I have to communicate to your Excellency, that we had a very serious alarm from the Indians yesterday evening at three o'clock, in the field of Mr. John Rabun, which is between seven and eight miles below Hartford and immediately on the river – The said Rabun being in his field, three Indians arose out of the corn, and one of them fired on him and wounded him severely in the back – He immediately took to flight – The pursued him with the most horrid yells, and as he crossed the fence both the others fired on him and wounded him slightly in the shoulder. They continued to pursue him near his house, where he got his gun and would have fired on them but for the interference of his wife, who clung around him and prevented him.[17]*

The war party went on to raid two other homes before fading into the woods. Tooke sent a detachment of men in pursuit, but was not optimistic that the raiders could be caught. Georgians rightfully feared that more such attacks were coming and that the arrival of the British on the Apalachicola would soon leave the frontier settlements awash in a river of blood.[18]

In Florida, meanwhile, John Yellowhair reached the hidden Red Stick camps along the Choctawhatchee and Yellow Water Rivers as these activities were taking place in Georgia. He found the surviving Red Sticks in desperate straits. The Spanish in Pensacola did not have the means to feed them and starvation was stalking the hidden camps. Untold numbers of men, women and children died in the swamps during the summer of 1814, their bones lost there to time and the elements. Detachments of U.S. soldiers, Choctaw warriors and Creeks loyal to the Big Warrior stalked the Red Sticks as well. Both British and American reports indicate that some of these parties were guided by the former Red Stick leader William Weatherford. He and Major Joseph Carson operated with impunity within miles of Pensacola, ignoring the sovereignty of Spain.[19]

Josiah Francis and Peter McQueen were in Pensacola when Henry Durgen arrived there to report the British landing on the Apalachicola. With his help they immediately addressed a letter to Captain Woodbine:

Our case is really miserable and lamentable, driven from House and Home without Food and Clothes to cover our Bodies by disasters and an Enemy, who has sworn our ruin, and hovering about Pensacola and Vicinity, where we can get no assistance, as the Spanish Government tells us that it is scarcely able to support its own troops.[20]

Durgen had arrived aboard the British warship HMS *Cockchafer*. Fearful of the disaster that would follow if the American cavalry known to be operating up the Escambia River found the hidden camps of his followers, the Prophet Francis sent word for his people to begin an overland journey to the Apalachicola River. He then boarded the warship as it weighed anchor for the same destination. The prophet's departure was observed by an American citizen who was in Pensacola on business:

The schooner Cock Chaffer, Captain Jackson, of forty men and five guns, left this place for Appalachicola, with Francis the prophet on board, on the 18th, at the time times was brought in by the Indians of the 39th regiment being in the rear of Pensacola. A Spanish brig from the Havanna is now in sight. The vessel is just going off – for further particulars I refer you to my next.[21]

McQueen followed on board a second vessel as more than 1,000 Red Stick refugees began making their way overland to Prospect Bluff. The walk must have been one of incredible misery. Starving, powerless and pursued by their enemies, the displaced Creeks traveled through the pine woods and dense river swamps with little food and in the hottest season of the year.

---

[1] Capt. George Woodbine, Talk to Council of Chiefs, May 28, 1814, Cochrane Papers (Given at Prospect Bluff).

[2] Capt. George Woodbine to Capt. Hugh Pigot, May 25, 1814, Cochrane Papers (Actually edited and signed at Prospect Bluff on May 28, 1814).

[3] Capt. George Woodbine to Lt. David Hope, HMS *Shelburne*, May 31, 1814, Cochrane Papers.

[4] *Ibid.*

[5] *Ibid.*

[6] *Ibid.*
[7] Tustunnuggee Thlucco, Tustunnuggee Hopoi and John Stedham to Col. Benjamin Hawkins, June 13, 1814, Hargrett Rare Book and Manuscript Library, The University of Georgia Libraries, Telamon Cuyler, box 77, folder 33, document 23.
[8] *Ibid.*
[9] Cappachimico (Kinhijee) to the Lower Creek Chiefs, undated, enclosed in *Ibid.*
[10] *Ibid.*
[11] Benjamin Hawkins, "Report of supplies to the Indians by the British and Spaniards at Pensacola and mouth of Chattahochie," received by Governor Peter Early on June 17, 1814, published in the *Georgia Journal*, June 22, 1814.
[12] *Ibid.*
[13] *Ibid.*
[14] *Ibid.*
[15] Benjamin Hawkins to the Big Warrior, Little Prince and other chiefs, June 16, 1814, *American State Papers: Indian Affairs*, Volume I, p. 845.
[16] Timothy Barnard to Mr. Munford, August 5, 1814, Hargrett Rare Book and Manuscript Library, The University of Georgia Libraries, Telamon Cuyler Collection, box 01, folder 11, document 15.
[17] Lt. Col. Allen Tooke to Gov. Peter Early, August 6, 1814, published in the *Georgia Journal*, August 10, 1814, p. 3.
[18] *Ibid.*
[19] Extract of letter from Camp Jackson to Charleston, April 17, 1814, *New Jersey Journal*, May 31, 1814, p. 2; Col. J.A. Pearson to Gov. William Hawkins, June 1, 12 and 13, 1814.
[20] Joshua [sic.] Francis and others to British Commander at St. George's Island, June 9, 1814, Cochrane Papers.
[21] Extract of a letter from a gentleman at Pensacola to his correspondent in New Orleans, July 25, 1814, *Louisiana Gazette*, August 16, 1814.

THREE

The British had been on the Apalachicola roughly six weeks when Captain Woodbine decided to strike hard against the Americans. Sergeant Smith, from his position at the head of the river, had been able to obtain specific intelligence on the strengths and weaknesses of the American forts higher up the Chattahoochee and Flint Rivers. Most of the Seminoles and Red Sticks in the immediate vicinity were now armed with modern British weaponry and Smith was anxious to try his hand against the Americans. He proposed to Woodbine that he and Corporal Denny be allowed to lead a strike against the frontier and the captain agreed that the time had come for action. The target was to be Fort Hawkins in Georgia and in particular Colonel Benjamin Hawkins, the U.S. Agent for Indian affairs, and his family:

> *The enterprize you have solicited my permission to undertake, I have from your representation of the practicability thereof consented to your attempted. But recollect to temper that laudable ambition you have to distinguish yourself in some dashing affair with prudence, and use every endeavour to obtain correct information of the strength of the object of attack. Should you succeed, I know I need scarcely inform you that "Humanity is the first quality in a truly brave man."[1]*

The destruction of Fort Hawkins and capture or killing of Colonel Hawkins would have been a symbolic stroke the likes of which had never been seen on the Southern frontier. Even the Red Stick capture of Fort Mims in 1813 would pale in comparison to it. Fort Hawkins, however, was no Fort Mims. Whereas the Alabama fort had been a hastily constructed stockade build during an

33

emergency by frontier settlers and militia with little if any military training, the Georgia outpost was a regularly built U.S. military installation. Located atop a high hill overlooking the Ocmulgee River at present-day Macon, Georgia, it had strong walls, stout blockhouses on diagonal corners and was garrisoned by regular U.S. Army troops. Smith and Denny could probably field an effective force of warriors by that point, all well-equipped with small arms, but they had no cannon with which to batter down the walls of the fort. Their likelihood of success was minimal at best.

Captain Woodbine authorized the attack and even gave the two non-commissioned officers temporary promotions to acting lieutenant, but he also expressed concern for the fate of Hawkins' family should the operation succeed:

The Indians will spare as few as possible but impress it on the minds of the party that accompany you that prisoners are my object, and that I set my face against putting any one not resisting to death or scalping them, and that according to the humanity they shew, so will you report their conduct to me and procure them rewards accordingly. Should any females (of which I understand the Colonels family are likely to be part) fall into your hand, you too well know the duty of an Englishman and a soldier to require my saying a word to you on the line of conduct to pursue.[2]

The attack would be the first major effort carried out by the force being organized at the forks of the Chattahoochee and Flint Rivers. The numbers of warriors available to Smith and Denny are unclear, but the British had distributed around 1,400 muskets from the storehouses at Prospect Bluff thus far, along with bayonets, ammunition and other supplies. The villages contributing warriors to the strike force likely would have included the Perryman towns of Tocktoethla and Tellmochesses as well as Ekanachatte (Red Ground), Tutalosi Talofa (Fowltown), Ocheesee Talofa, Tomathli, Okitiyakani, Blunt's Town, Hyhappo. Miccosukee and Tallahassee Talofa may have been included, but documentation suggests that Cappachimico was still trying to keep both sides happy at this point.

No sooner had Woodbine authorized the raid, however, than did news arrive of a developing situation in Pensacola:

...For some days past it had been pretty well understood that six hundred Americans were posted at the head of the River Scambia about 25 miles from this place, that the Americans and Indians were very near this place, supposed by some to take possession, by others, that this was not intended, but committing depredations and murdering &c. &c. This morning I find the facts to be these – A party of American horsemen about 40 (no Choctaws) headed by Colonel Carson, and joined by Wm. Weatherford an Indian chief, are pursuing the Creek Indians and are killing them wherever they meet them. They were yesterday at Mr. Marshalls about 16 miles off the other side of this Bay, and killed 7 or 8 Indians there. They then went to Mr. Miller's Plantation, but did no damage there.[3]

Colonel Joseph Carson and William Weatherford were also reported to have attacked Red Stick refugees on the Conecuh River and an American force was reported to be gathering at the head of the Escambia for a strike against Pensacola. Meanwhile, Andrew Jackson was reported to be assembling an army of 9,500 men for an attack against the British and their allies on the Apalachicola.[4]

The intelligence came from an anonymous source in Pensacola, but one who had clearly attached himself to the British cause. Some of the information in the report was accurate while some, as the source himself observed, was undoubtedly exaggerated:

...My own belief is, that half this number of men [i.e. 9,500] are not as yet collected into one body in this neighbourhood, nor do I think that the Americans will dare to attack this place, at the same time there is no accounting for the acts of madmen I observe. Marshall's Plantation is in Spanish Territory. Wm. Weatherford was lately fighting alongside of McQueen, and has given himself up to the Americans.[5]

Woodbine had already planned to proceed in person to Pensacola to meet with the Red Stick chiefs there in person. He now decided to go there without delay. Before heading down to St. Joseph Bay where a British warship was waiting, he recalled Smith and Denny from their planned attack on Fort Hawkins:

You will instead of proceeding on the intended enterprize immediately place yourself at the head of at least three hundred picked men, and march with all possible speed to Pensacola and there join me for an attack on the place we mentioned.

Secrecy and dispatch is requisite. Take Col. Perryman, Ben Perryman, Fulsahlanny and the Burgesses with you – and all volunteers let them be able men. Tallafaggys cattle will follow you (Daniel comes up to you, as quick as possible). George Perryman I am obliged to take with e as the business requires the best interpreter. Now is your time to make a dash! I will give you every chance. Keep your journal.[6]

The objective of the new attack envisioned by the captain and evidently already discussed with Lieutenant Smith was to be the city of Mobile itself. A report dispatched to Admiral Alexander Cochrane by Woodbine off Cape San Blas on July 25, 1814, indicated that he planned to remain in Pensacola only a short time and then return to the Apalachicola. Circumstances would intervene, however, and British efforts on the river would stagnate for several months while they attempted to create order from the chaos then reining at the extreme western end of Northwest Florida.[7]

As these events were taking place on the Apalachicola River and in Pensacola, news reached the United States that a massive British fleet was assembling in the Caribbean for a planned strike against the Gulf Coast. Captain Parker McCrabb, an American merchantman fresh from Havana, arrived in St. Mary's, Georgia, in early August with firsthand information on the growing British threat. He had seen a colonel of the Royal Marines in Cuba and reported that the officer was on the way to Florida with arms, ammunition and other supplies to be used in arming the Creek Indians for operations against the United States.[8]

The colonel of Marines mentioned in the report was Brevet Major Edward Nicolls of the Royal Marines, who would assume the local rank of lieutenant colonel upon his arrival in Florida. A respected and seasoned officer, Nicolls had taken part in fighting around the world and his body bore the scars of numerous wounds. Dubbed "Fighting Nicolls" by those who knew him, he had been picked by Admiral Cochrane to take charge of the Indian and Colonial Marines force being raised by Captain Woodbine.

. A second account from St. Mary's, attributed to a "gentleman of undoubted veracity," relayed additional information from the same source about the British plans and identified the warships that sailed for Florida as the HMS *Hermes* and HMS *Charon*:

The colonel commanding dined at a public table – he spoke freely of great cruelties committed by the troops under General Jackson during his expedition against the Indians; and seemed exasperated against the Americans. – He urged that the country belonged to the Indians – they were the first settlers, and it was his intention to restore it to them. His first stand would be at Colerain in Georgia, and from thence to Savannah. The colonel reported that he expected a reinforcement of 4000 men – that he had on board the two ships 3000 uniforms, epaulets, swords, &c. for officers whom he intended to commission. A gentleman who was on board the Hermes read one of the proclamations signed by colonel Woodbine inviting all classes and descriptions of people to the British standard for protection and freedom.[9]

Nicolls reached the Apalachicola River on August 12, 1814, to find that chaos and a potential humanitarian crisis were building in Northwest Florida:

We arrived here this morning, and lost no time in disembarking the men on Vincent Island, but did not land the stores. I ordered the men to build strong Hutts, and continue to do so until I returned. Captain Percy and myself went off the same day for the bluff, but owing to the stupidity of a guide given to us by Captain Umpherville we were lead astray for two days and oliged to return for a supply of provisions, our next attempt was fortunate, on my arrival at the luff I found Captain Woodbine had gone to Pensacola, that the Sergeant and Corporal were up in the nation drilling the men, and that for want of provisions, they could not assemble, that the upper town Creeks had been driven from their homes, and everything they possessed taken from them, as they had no arms to resist, and in consequence of their coming in such numbers upon Perryman and Capachamico, they had created a famine, and were actually eating the corn before it was ripe.[10]

Nicolls' seems at this stage to have been unaware that Smith and Denny had been ordered to Pensacola by Captain Woodbine. Despite his reputation as

37

a "blustering Irishman" and combat officer, the colonel possessed a soft heart for those less fortunate than himself. He was appalled by the condition of the Red Stick Creeks that he saw at Prospect Bluff, noting that they looked more like skeletons than human beings:

...About 50 Warriors and 30 women and children came to the Bluff for arms, such objects I never saw the like of, absolute skin and bone, but cheerfull and resolved to do their utmost against the common enemy. An old man told me, when I asked him how far it was to where the enemy were, and if he knew the way to lead me to them, he said it was seven days Journey to them, (about 300 miles) that he could not miss the way, for it was marked by the graves of his five children.[11]

Colonel Nicolls related that the old man was grateful for the new musket given to him by the British but even more so for the bayonet to attach to it. The warrior observed that "he always thought something was wanting." "Now that he had a bayonet," he told Nicolls, "he would rush on the Americans, when he was sure of victory."[12]

The two British officers did not remain long at Prospect Bluff, but returned to Apalachicola Bay where they encountered small schooners chartered by Woodbine to retrieve the 600 muskets still in the storehouses and carry them to Pensacola:

...We only staid eight hours at the bluff, my intention when I left it, was to bring up everything and fortify the place, as strong as circumstances would permit, detach the greater part of the officers and men, to drill the Indians, and wait untill I got provisions, as we could not assemble more than my own number, untill we were supplied, but on our return, we had the pleasure of getting a letter from Captain Woodbine at Pensacola, informing us of the Governor's request to land there for the defence of the place, and that he had sent two Schooners to bring everything from the bluff, particularly 600 stand of arms, but as I saw, and was informed, that partys of 30 and 40 men, were coming in daily for arms to the bluff, from a great distance, I deemed it proper not to take away the 600 stand, as they might think we were not sincere in our promises, and return disappointed.[13]

Spain had declared its neutrality in the conflict then raging between the United States and Great Britain, even though U.S. forces had taken the Spanish city of Mobile the previous year. With rumors abounding that the Americans planned to do the same to Pensacola, Governor Mateo Gonzales Manrique was desperate for assistance and offered to let the British and their allies occupy the city without waiting for the approval of his superiors.

Pensacola was a relatively small city in 1814 and, with the probable exception of Fort San Carlos de Barrancas, its defenses were weak. The entrance to the harbor was defended by the log fort at the Barrancas and its masonry water battery, but the city itself was protected only by Fort San Miguel and a couple of blockhouses. The fort dated from before the American Revolution and was in a decrepit condition with sections missing from its walls. It was dangerously exposed to fire from nearby heights, as the British had learned when they tried to defend it against attacking Allied forces during the Revolutionary War. The Spanish garrison was small and morale was low.

The governor was so overjoyed to see British ships appear in the harbor that he immediately offered to place the city and its defenses in Captain Woodbine's hands:

I am preparing every possible mode of defense. With the Indians I am levelling a high hill, formerly a Fort (was constructed on it,) that commands the principal Fort (St. Michael) of this town, and am repairing it also, it being much out of order. The Governor has requested me to take possession of it, and defend the Town, which I will do with a body of white men, mulattoes & blacks that I am raising here, and encamp the Indians round it. The Governor proposes retreating to Fort Barrancas, which commands the entrance of the Harbour, and to leave the protection of the Town to me. He has desired me to do as I please either in destroying or erecting Forts.[14]

Nicolls joined him there on August 23, 1814, and with the permission of the Governor landed his force of Royal Marines in the city and raised the English flag over Fort St. Michael alongside that of Spain. It did not take long for American authorities to learn that British troops were in Pensacola:

We have this moment received the following information from a Mr. John Morris, who has just arrived from the neighborhood of Pensacola, he left there three days ago. He states that about ten days ago, some British officers called the Indians together, about a mile or two out of town, and gave them a talk; (no Americans, and but a few Spaniards were permitted to hear it) the Indians say that the British directs them not to kill women and children. They say that a number of the British were expected at Pensacola every day, and when they arrived, they should be supplied with arms, ammunition, and provisions. Two British vessels were said to have arrived the day before he, (Morris) came away. They are daily mustering, parading, and exercising the Indians, which seems to be very disgusting to them.[15]

This intelligence was forwarded to U.S. District Judge Harry Toulmin by the Pierce brothers, who owned a mill near the ruins of Fort Mims. Judge Toulmin immediately warned Governor Willie Blunt of Tennessee that the Red Sticks knew the weakness of the posts and settlements north of Mobile and that repeats of the disaster at Fort Mims could be expected unless action was taken to improve the defenses of the frontier.[16]

To bolster the seaward defenses of Mobile, American troops were pushing forward the completion of Fort Bowyer. A semi-circular fort armed with heavy cannon to command the pass leading from the Gulf of Mexico into Mobile Bay, Bowyer stood on the present site of Fort Morgan. While many believed that a British naval attack would blow to bits the defenses of wood and sand, Major William Lawrence and his men of the 2nd U.S. Infantry determined to stand their ground. The British at Pensacola, meanwhile, decided to attack.

---

[1] Capt. George Woodbines to Acting Lt. Samuel Smith, July 21, 1814, Cochrane Papers.
[2] *Ibid.*
[3] Unknown Informant to Lt. Jackson, HMS *Cockchafer*, July 19, 1814, Cochrane Papers.
[4] *Ibid.*
[5] *Ibid.*
[6] Capt. George Woodbine to Acting Lieutenant Samuel Smith, July 22, 1814, Cochrane Papers.
[7] Captain George Woodbine to Admiral Alexander Cochrane, July 25, 1814, Cochrane Papers.
[8] Abraham Bessent to Gov. Peter Early, August 20, 1814, Hargrett Rare Book and Manuscript Library, The University of Georgia Libraries, Telamon Cuyler Collection, Box 04, Document 04.

[9] Report from St. Mary's dated August 25, 1814, published in the *Georgia Journal*, September 7, 1814, p. 2.

[10] Bvt. Major Edward Nicolls to Admiral Alexander Cochrane, August 12, 1814, Cochrane Papers.

[11] *Ibid.*

[12] *Ibid.*

[13] *Ibid.*

[14] Capt. George Woodbine to Admiral Alexander Cochrane, August 9, 1814, Cochrane Papers.

[15] W. & J. Pierce to Hon. Harry Toulmin, August 5, 1814, published in the *Western Monitor*, September 9, 1814, p. 2.

[16] Hon. Harry Toulman to Gov. Willie Blunt, August 14, 1814, published in the *Western Monitor*, September 9, 1814, p. 2.

FOUR

The British attacked Fort Bowyer on the afternoon of September 15, 1814. Captain William Henry Percy of the Royal Navy led his squadron of four ships against the fort while Captains Robert Henry and George Woodbine attacked from land with 60 British marines and 130 Creek and Seminole warriors. Lieutenant Colonel Nicolls was severely ill and did not accompany the land force into the battle, although he did fight with considerable bravery from the decks of HMS *Hermes.* The fort on Mobile Point was defended by a mere 120 men from the 2nd U.S. Infantry under Major William Lawrence:

...[A]t 4 P.M. we opened our battery, which was returned from two ships, and two brigs, as they approached. The action became general at about 20 minutes past 4, and was continued without intermission on either side until 7, when one ship and 2 brigs were compelled to retire. The leading ship, supposed to be the Commodore, mounting twenty-two 32-pound carronades, having anchored nearest to our battery, was so much disabled, her cable being cut by our shot, that she drifted on shore, within 600 yards of the battery, and the other vessels having got out of our reach, we kept such a tremendous fire upon her that she was set on fire and abandoned by the few of the crew who survived. At 10 P.M. we had the pleasure of witnessing the explosion of her magazine.[1]

The British ship lost in the attack on Fort Bowyer was the *Hermes.* Problems with the wind made her difficult to steer and she ran aground within almost point blank range of the American guns. The other vessels managed to get out of range, although they sustained damage as well. American casualties totaled only 4 killed and 5 wounded. The British, on the other hand, lost 32 killed and 40 wounded. Among the latter was Colonel Nicolls himself:

...I had the misfortune to be wounded by a grape shot, in the right eye and temple, which has deprived me of its sight, and obliged me to go below for a few minutes to get it dressed. When I came up again, I got slightly wounded in the leg, and knocked down by a Splinter which struck me on the back of my head, I remained untill Captain Percy sent me with the rest of the wounded on board the other ships.[2]

The loss of the *Hermes* was a disaster for the British, but their failure to take Fort Bowyer led to an even greater problems. Spain had declared its neutrality in the conflict and the use of Pensacola as a base for such an attack was a serious violation of international law. Major General Andrew Jackson was infuriated and retaliated by striking at Pensacola in early November:

...On Sunday the 6th inst. Our army approached it, and a flag was sent in, summoning a surrender – but from the reception it met with, the fire of six or eight round of cannon, it could not make the demand, but was forced to retreat – as it was very late in the evening when the flag was sent, the matter was deferred for adjustment until morning after Reveilee "to arms" was beat; in a few minutes the army entered the town in triumph under a brisk fire of grape and canister from the town, and bomb and ball from the fort and some British vessels that lay at anchor in the Bay. We, however, sustained but little injury.[3]

The British withdrew in frustration after Governor Mateo Gonzales Manrique refused to place his troops under their command or do much to prepare the city for defense. Colonel Nicolls fought a brief delaying action before evacuating his marines to the ships in the harbor. His Creek and Seminole allies had been carried across Pensacola Bay before Jackson's arrival. They were ordered to proceed overland to the Apalachicola while the Royal Navy covered their retreat.

Nicolls and other officers had threatened to level Pensacola with cannon fire when American troops occupied the city, but they ceased firing as soon as U.S. soldiers entered populated areas. From the bay the British watched as Jackson's men occupied Fort St. Michael and raised the Star-Spangled Banner over the old Spanish city. Shore parties blew up Fort San Carlos de Barrancas to prevent its occupation by the Americans, more or less forcefully embarking the 180-200 Spanish troops from its garrison with a promise to deliver them to Cuba.

The destruction of the fort at the Barrancas made it impossible for Jackson to defend Pensacola against a naval attack so he withdrew back to Mobile within a few days. Major Uriah Blue of the 39th U.S. Infantry was sent at the head of a force of Choctaw warriors and Tennessee volunteers to destroy the retreating Red Sticks and drive the British from the Apalachicola. The famed frontiersman David Crockett was one of the soldiers in Blue's command. He described in his autobiography how the column had some success but ultimately ran low on food and had to give up the push to the Apalachicola. Major Blue divided his force sending the Tennesseans north into Alabama while he retreated west with the rest of his men. Both forces reached the frontier settlements on the verge of starvation.

The British set sail for Apalachicola Bay. Their plan to take Mobile had been a dismal failure but they still fostered hopes for successful operations against the Georgia frontier. With a major army coming under Major General Sir Edward Pakenham and Admiral Alexander Cochrane, they knew that the war on the Gulf Coast was far from over.

In Georgia, Colonel Benjamin Hawkins recognized this as well. Although he was the U.S. Agent for Indian Affairs and no longer a military officer, Hawkins called on the U.S.-allied warriors of the primary Creek Nation for help. He planned to make Coweta his headquarters and announced he was calling out the Yuchis under Captain Timpoochee Barnard to protect the frontier from a point 20 miles south of Fort Lawrence. Aumuccullee's chiefs were asked to station warriors another 30 miles to the south as a scouting force to watch for signs of Red Stick activity. Hawkins also asked Governor Peter Early to have the militia officers at the Creek Agency act under his command.[4]

Hawkins warned Governor Early that the danger from the Seminoles and Red Sticks was growing "as the British force will be ready to act with them." He urged the governor to call up 500 mounted militia to join with regular forces in an operation to "crush those people."[5]

As he was making his plans for defending the frontier, Hawkins received word that a British officer, apparently either acting Lieutenant Samuel Smith or Woodbine himself, had returned from Pensacola to the vicinity of the forks of the Chattahoochee and Flint Rivers. According to informants, the officer was at the town of Thomas Perryman and had announced that a large number of refugee slaves from Georgia was expected to join the British ranks within the month. Colonel Hawkins warned that action should be taken immediately lest the entire frontier be exposed.[6]

As was noted in Chapter One, Perryman's town of Tocktoethla then stood on the Georgia side of the Chattahoochee about 10 miles above the forks. According to Creek chiefs allied with the United States, it was the center of the pro-British forces while Cappachimico of Miccosukee was working quietly to restrain war parties intent on striking the Georgia settlements. He had been offered $100 for every trader, beef contractor or other American found in Creek or Seminole territory and a similar sum for any slaves that could be captured and brought in to enlist in the British forces. Cappachimico had answered, however, for the British to begin the war and he would decide what to do at that point. Meanwhile, two war parties were peacefully turned back by the Aumuccullee chiefs and another group of Creek leaders near Kinnard's on the Flint River.[7]

Confusion in the borderlands. The chiefs and leading warriors of some Creek and Seminole towns committed to join the British while others emulated Cappachimico's position and maintained their neutrality. The Little Prince of the Lower Creeks committed his warriors to the United States and ordered that any warriors allied with Nicolls and Woodbine leave the Nation:

...You have now heard the Talks. All those who are not now willing to protect their own nation will be considered as hostile to the U.S. I have now thrown away the Siminolies. We shall now have to go to war against them. I do not understand what you Cussetaus are about, or what you intend to do. You must now say quickly what you mean to do. There is no time to be considering on it now. If you are or the British, say so.[8]

Christian Limbaugh, a paid assistant to Colonel Hawkins, reported that the Chattahoochee River towns from Eufaula north had attended the "Grand Council of the friendly Chiefs." The Cussetas were almost unanimous for continuing their alliance with the United States. Major William McIntosh, the war chief of that town, had fought alongside Andrew Jackson during the Creek War of 1813-1814 and was asked to assemble the warriors of the Lower Creek towns for a campaign against the British.[9]

The British, meanwhile, moved almost immediately upon their return from Pensacola to start the construction of the fort known today as Nicolls' Outpost. The first specific reference its building appeared in a report from the Tallassee chief Lieutenant Lewis who was raising a force of warriors to assist in the developing American campaign down the Apalachicola:

Lieut. Lewis writes from Fort Jackson on the 14ᵗʰ that several British troops and most of the hostile Indians from Pensacola had arrived at the junction of Flint and Chatahooche rivers, with the view of building a Fort there. He also states that the enemy are ready to march against us at a short notice, and that they have spies constantly out to report from time to time the strength of our garrisons.[10]

On the same day that Lieutenant Lewis penned his report, November 14, 1814, three confidential informants testified at Timothy Barnard's trading post on the Flint River giving details of the British plan of attack. The first part of this was the sending out of the war party from Tocktoethla that had been turned back by the Aumucculle chiefs, although a few continued onward and stole six horses from Timothy Barnard and four from the Creek Agency. A second similar movement was halted in favor of a new plan. According to a Creek chief whose nephew was with the British, the plan was for the warriors to wait until the Georgia militia marching to reinforce Andrew Jackson had passed through the Nation. Once the soldiers were too far away to render assistance to the frontiers, the Red Sticks and Seminoles would strike. The target would be the settled area east of Fort Hawkins and they were to bring in as many horses and slaves as possible.[11]

The reports of both sides from this period mention British plans to capture and liberate slaves. Nicolls and Woodbine were realizing solid success in finding black recruits for their new battalion of Colonial Marines. Many African and African-American slaves from both Pensacola and adjacent American territory had enlisted in the battalion, as had free blacks from the coastal areas. Others had come down the Apalachicola from Georgia to obtain their freedom at Prospect Bluff.

The British spent late November building two forts on the Apalachicola River. The lower one was usually referred to as the "British Post" and stood adjacent to the John Forbes & Company store at Prospect Bluff. It consisted of a riverfront water battery and an octagonal magazine and was surrounded by a bastioned entrenchment with a light palisade. The post was clearly intended for use as a supply depot where arms, ammunition and other material coming up the Apalachicola River from Royal Navy ships in the Gulf could be stored until boats and canoes could carry it up the river to the upper fort at the confluence of the Chattahoochee and Flint River. It also would provide a place of safety for

47

the wives and children of the warriors and Colonial Marines as the campaign against Georgia went forward.

The upper fort, Nicolls' Outpost, was a rectangular earthen redoubt built atop one of the large Mississippian Indian mounds at today's River Landing Park in Chattahoochee. A ditch ringed the structure, the earth from which had been thrown up to form the ramparts of the fort. An exterior picket work or light stockade surrounded both the ditch and redoubt. This additional defense was probably built with the sharpened points of the logs pointing outward at an angle to deter infantry attacks instead of straight up in the air as such stockades are often pictured. Two pieces of artillery – a 24-pounder cohorn mortar and a 5 ½-inch brass howitzer – were mounted inside the redoubt.

The location of the fort atop the prehistoric mound protected it from river flooding, which is common along the Apalachicola in winter and spring. It also placed the walls about 15 feet above the surrounding terrain, an elevation that improved the defensibility of the redoubt. It was thought for many years that Nicolls' Outpost might have stood atop the high bluffs at Chattahoochee, but British reports describe its location as having been "atop a mount immediately upon the banks of the river." A visiting French nobleman, the Comte de Castelnau, visited the river landing area during the 1830s and reported seeing "evidently modern" entrenchments atop an "enormous tumuli" there. Although Castelnau's account has often been interpreted to state that the "tumuli" or mound was 180 feet high, an inspection of the original French manuscript reveals that the comte actually wrote that the mound was 18-feet high. The latter elevation is much more in keeping with the heights of the larger mounds at Chattahoochee Landing.[12]

The fort itself was surrounded by the camps of the Red Stick Creek and Seminole warriors who had allied themselves with the British. Since winter was approaching, they likely built huts or cabins to protect themselves from the elements. Most of the arms previously stockpiled at Thomas Perryman's town were moved down to the new fort even as canoes and boats continued to make runs down the Apalachicola River to bring more weaponry up to the outpost. Food was in short supply, although the warriors and troops at Nicolls' Outpost likely did not suffer from hunger to the degree of those down the river at Prospect Bluff. The proximity of numerous large Creek and Seminole villages allowed for a more reliable supply of provisions. Warriors also went out into the woods in search of deer and other game.

As November 1814 came to an end, the British were firmly in place on the Apalachicola River and working to complete their forts at both Prospect Bluff and the forks. The main British fleet would soon arrive in the northern Gulf of Mexico, bringing with it thousands of troops for the planned attack on New Orleans. Jackson's capture of Pensacola aside, the Americans remained largely on the defensive, watching and waiting to see the strategy of the British and their allies unfold.

---

[1] Major William Lawrence to Major General Andrew Jackson, September 15, 1814, republished in *The Cabinet*, October 26, 1814, p. 3.

[2] Lt. Col. Edward Nicolls to Admiral Alexander Cochrane, August-November 1814, Cochrane Papers.

[3] Thomas A. Rogers, Letter dated at St. Stephens, Alabama, November 13, 1814, *Dedham Gazette*, December 23, 1814, p. 3.

[4] Col. Benjamin Hawkins to Gov. Peter Early, November 3, 1814, Hargrett Rare Book and Manuscript Libraries, The University of Georgia Libraries, Telamon Cuyler Collection, Box 76, Folder 25, Document 12.

[5] *Ibid.*

[6] Col. Benjamin Hawkins to Gov. Peter Early, November 5, 1814, Hargrett Rare Book and Manuscript Libraries, The University of Georgia Libraries, Telamon Cuyler Collection, Box 76, Folder 25, Document 14.

[7] Chiefs to Col. Benjamin Hawkins, November 11, 1814, enclosed in Hawkins to Early, November 15, 1814.

[8] Talk of Little Prince at Coweta, November 1814, published in the *Georgia Journal*, November 23, 1814, pp. 2-3.

[9] *Ibid.*

[10] *Georgia Journal*, November 23, 1814, pp. 2-3.

[11] Statement of "three confidential people" interviewed at Timothy Barnard's and interpreted by him, November 14, 1814, included in Hawkins to Early, November 15, 1814).

[12] Lt. Col. Edward Nicolls to Capt. Robert Henry, December 5, 1814, original document in Carswell Collection; Francis de Laporte, comte de Castelnau,, *Vues et Souvenirs de L'Amerique de Nord*I, Chez Arthus Bertrand, Paris, 1842.

FIVE

The small war parties sent by the British in November 1814 to scout and raid along the Georgia frontier had an alarming impact on settlers and military leaders alike. In addition to the hundreds of allied Creeks ordered into the field by Colonel Hawkins, militia cavalry companies were called out by Governor Peter Early. Several of these cooperated with the Yuchi under Captain Timpoochee Barnard to penetrate as far as the Creek town of Chehaw west of the Flint River.

Led by Lieutenant Colonel Peter Tooke, the force marked a new trail connecting the Hartford and Chehaw trails and then followed the latter path to the Flint River at a point 23 miles upstream from the principal Chehaw town. The soldiers crossed over and marched south to the town, where Tooke, Barnard and several other officers went in alone to meet with the chiefs and principal warriors.[1]

The council lasted for about three hours, as Colonel Took asked the Chehaws to keep a watch on the frontiers and spread the alarm at the first appearance of the British or their allied warriors. He also asked for their assistance in operations against the British when the necessity arose. The Chehaw chiefs wavered on the subject of providing military assistance to the Americans. They had no interest in sending their young men to war, "wishing to remain friendly to both sides." The chiefs did agree to send eight of their number as emissaries to the towns that had allied with the British to learn what they could about future movements and plans.[2]

Colonel Tooke went on to mention that Georgia or U.S. forces might cut a road through Creek lands to the junction of the Chattahoochee and Flint Rivers. They did not respond. British supplies and sentiment were evident among the men of Chehaw and two other nearby towns. Muskets and ammunition could be seen everywhere and the warriors did not deny that they had received them from the British at Thomas Perryman's town. While some of the chiefs and warriors he met appeared to be truly friendly to the United States, Tooke believed that others only gave the appearance of being so because of the size of the military force with him.[3]

The Georgia troops returned to Hartford, which they thought was 60-70 miles from Chehaw. The forks of the Chattahoochee and Flint they believed was another 80 miles or so. Tooke recommended the immediate opening of a road from Hartford to the Flint River near Chehaw, "there to erect and establish a Military Post." Governor Early accepted this suggestion and the troops of Brigadier General David Blackshear would build Fort Early at the recommended site later during the winter.[4]

The scout by the militia and Yuchi companies was the first serious field movement by Georgia authorities in defense of their frontier against the British. As Governor Early and others worked to put more troops in the field, Colonel Hawkins reported that 263 warriors had enrolled thus far in the Creek companies he was raising. Eighty of these were the Yuchis under Timpoochee Barnard and the others consisted of 71 Tuckabatchees under Lieutenant Lewis along with 112 Lower Creeks enrolled by Christian Limbaugh.[5]

The Indian agent felt that he would have a full regiment of 700-800 allied Creeks ready to operate against the British, Seminoles and Red Sticks by the end of November. We was still waiting for expected instructions from General Jackson as late as November 15, 1814, but was already recommending the construction of bateaux for the trip down the Chattahoochee River to attack Nicolls' Outpost. These boats would be built in Creek style, made from two trees with a batten piece about one-foot wide to connect them and form a boat. They could be propelled using either oars or poles.[6]

It is clear from his reports that Colonel Hawkins visualized a campaign against the Apalachicola River forts in which his Creeks would be joined by either militia or regular troops or both. It would be a major undertaking, as Captain Robert Henry of the Royal Marines reported from Prospect Bluff on November 22, 1814, that 1,100 warriors, 450 women and 750 children were then at the British Post. Another 500 additional Creeks had just arrived "from the American lines," but he did not say how many of these new arrivals were warriors. The numbers do not appear to have included the several hundred Creeks already at Nicolls' Outpost.[7]

New intelligence on the British activities continued to reach American authorities. Timpoochee Barnard returned to the Creek Agency on the night of December 2 and reported that the delegation of Chehaw chiefs had returned from their visit to the lower towns. The chiefs had tried to intervene in the "dances" taking place in these villages, an evident reference to the "Dance of the Indians of the Lakes" which had become an important war ceremony among the Red Sticks during the Creek War of 1813-1814. It had been introduced to them by the Shawnee. The Prophet Josiah Francis was one of its key proponents.[8]

The Chehaw chiefs warned the men of the lower towns that they were "all going to run mad" as they felt many of the Upper Creeks had done when the Red Stick movement spread through the Alabama towns in 1813. Thomas Perryman was back at Tocktoethla near the forks and the chiefs had seen a British officer there who "told them if they did not go and spill blood he would take from them all his guns again."[9]

Barnard went on to report that many of the slaves of the traders living along the Flint River had escaped and "all gone to some fort," undoubtedly a reference to either Nicolls' Outpost and/or the Post at Prospect Bluff. A number of slaves from the Creek Agency had joined them. Horses were also being stolen and carried to the British. The young war chief was accompanied by Uchee Mico, who joined him in asking that all of the Yuchis be placed under Barnard's command and that the United States supply them with provisions. Otherwise their warriors faced starvation and would not be able to guard the frontier.[10]

The lack of provisions was impacting the movements on both sides of the conflict. British reports from the Apalachicola River were filled with requests for additional food. Many of the Red Sticks had arrived in Florida too late in the year to make a crop. Others had seen their fields as far east as the Choctawhatchee River destroyed during Major Blue's expedition, which had itself been forced to turn back before reaching the Apalachicola due to near starvation.

This was the general situation on the frontier and at the forts on the Apalachicola when the main British force reached the Gulf Coast. Governor Early was alerted to the developing situation by Major General John McIntosh[*] who reported that the intelligence was brought by the noted frontiersman, Major Sam Dale, on December 11, 1814.

Dale reported that 50 or 60 British warships had arrived off the mouth of the Mississippi River – called the Belize – and that General Jackson had

---

[*] Note: There were two men named McIntosh involved in activities in Georgia at this point: Major William McIntosh, the mestizo war chief of Coweta, and Major General John McIntosh, a white general in the Georgia militia. This individual was the latter.

marched for New Orleans. Infantry from all directions was following him. Major Uriah Blue of the 39th U.S. Infantry was expected to march by New Year's with 1,500-1,600 mounted men as well as Choctaw, Chickasaw and allied Creek warriors to wipe out lingering parties of Red Sticks and attack the British on the Apalachicola. It was also reported that Lieutenant Carey of the U.S. Army was missing along with three men, a woman and a child. They had left Fort Jackson by water for Mobile, but had never arrived. A report was current that the woman and child showed up in Pensacola and reported that the lieutenant and other men had been killed. She was immediately set upon by Red Stick warriors and killed, along with her child.[11]

Reference has been made to Major Blue's expedition, which included another famed frontiersman, David Crockett. Distance, lack of supplies and the inability to communicate prevented Hawkins from cooperating with blue and the major was forced to withdraw after achieving minimal results.

Admiral Cochrane's flagship, HMS *Tonnant*, called at Apalachicola Bay on its way to the waters off New Orleans. Cappachimico, Thomas Perryman, the Prophet Francis and others were invited aboard to dine with the admiral and his senior officers. Some idea of the true opinions of these British officers about their American Indian allies can be found in a letter written by Cochrane's "fleet captain" and executive officer, future Admiral Sir Edward Codrington:

...We had the honour of these Majestic Beasts dining with us two days in the 'Tonnant,' and we are to be disgusted with a similar honour here to-day. All the body clothes they get they put on one over the other, except trowsers, which they consider as encumbrances it should seem in our way of using them, and they therefore tie them round their waists for the present, in order to convert them to leggings hereafter.[12]

Codrington went on to provide a rare eyewitness description of the practice of the Red Stick prophets of wearing the skin and feathers of birds as headdresses. U.S. battlefield accounts from the Creek War of 1813-1814 mention that prophets were often seen encouraging their warriors while wearing such plumage, but the British officer's account provides much more detail:

...Some of them appeared in their own picturesque dresses at first, with the skin of a handsome plumed bird on the head and arms; the bird's beak pointing down the forehead, the wings over the ears, and the tail down the poll. But they are now all in hats (some cocked, gold-laced ones), and I jackets such as are

worn by the sergeants in the Guards, and they have no the appearance of dressed-up apes.[13]

The obvious racism in Codrington's account aside, he likely was describing the Prophet Francis and his principal followers. Francis remained an important religious and political figure to the refugee Red Sticks at this point and probably was responsible for a number of the Lower Creek and Seminole towns taking up the red club and beginning the "Dance of the Indians of the Lakes." His star was once again ascending.

The Creek and Seminole leaders were invited by Admiral Cochrane to accompany the British to New Orleans, an offer that they accepted. The thinking behind this gesture was probably that the admiral expected the veteran troops of Lieutenant General Sir Edward Pakenham to make short work of Andrew Jackson's army. Seeing them easily vanquish the hero of Horseshoe Bend, the British must have thought, would inspire the Creeks and Seminoles to immediately rise up in force and attack the Georgia frontier. They would, of course, witness an entirely different spectacle on the field of Chalmette.

Admiral Cochrane also took advantage of the opportunity to release a printed broadside addressed to the "Great and Illustrious Chiefs of the Creek and other Indian Nations." The *Tonnant* was equipped with a printing press and the document, which invited the American Indians of the Southeast to join with the British who would help them to drive away the settlers and armies of the United States, was widely distributed. An original copy was later found by a missionary working in the Indian Nations of Oklahoma. It had been carefully preserved by the eldest daughter of the Prophet Francis.

The British made no secret of their arrival in force and officials in Georgia were quick to learn of their presence at the mouth of the Apalachicola. Some of the allied Creek chiefs relayed the intelligence to Colonel Hawkins and General John McIntosh on December 21, 1814:

...Yesterday, a dispatch was received by the Governor from Gen. M'Intosh, stating that information had been given by the Indians of the arrival at the mouth of the Apalachicola, in Florida, of a large British fleet, having on board, according to the enemy's statement, fourteen thousand troops and a considerable portion of them [negroes]. Seven of the vessels are said to be large, the remainder of smaller size, and are loaded with ammunition and presents for the Indians. The British have built a strong fort at Forbe's store,

and placed in it a garrison of 300 men. All the Indians have been invited to come and receive presents, the Redsticks and many [negroes] have gone.[14]

Even as fighting erupted on Lake Borgne and below New Orleans, the flood of Red Sticks, Lower Creeks, Seminoles and Africans arriving on the Apalachicola increased. By January 1815 the British were able to report that 3,381 warriors and 170 blacks were ready for action. The black men were recruits for the Colonial Marines, while the warriors included 1,421 men from the Apalachicola and lower Chattahoochee Rivers, 400 Lower Creeks from Chehaw and surrounding towns, 800 Red Sticks and 760 Seminoles or Miccosukees. Whether all of these individuals were actually on the Apalachicola is not clear, but the tally does provide a view of the size of the auxiliary force that Colonel Nicolls expected to carry with him as he advanced on the Georgia frontier after returning from New Orleans.[15]

Intelligence from an American spy, probably a Creek warrior, indicated that food stocks at the British forts were seriously depleted

...There are a few white troops at Forbes's store (18 miles up the Apalachicola on the East side). The store was surrounded with a ditch. Thirty-two warriors of Choctaws, from Fort Jackson (a part of those who had surrendered there) and a great many Red Clubs were there. The runaway and stolen negroes were close by the stor.; Provisions short - bisquit only. So great the scarcity of meat, that the Choctaws subsisted partly on stinking old cow hides.[16]

The informant reported that British troops could be seen landing "from the mouth of the river," a statement that probably indicates he had seen the operation underway to move supplies from the ships of the Royal Navy to the storehouses on St. Vincent Island. From there the material would be carried by boat and canoe up the river to Prospect Bluff.

More ominously, the report included information that the "chief warrior of Mic,co,soo,kee led a party of his warriors toward the frontiers of Georgia, ten in number, and killed five white people." According to the American spy, the raiding party had "carried the scalps to the British below the confluence of the Flint and Chattahoochie," an apparent reference to Nicolls' Outpost. The earlier efforts of Captain Woodbine to restrain his allies from scalping had apparently been forgotten.[17]

Colonel Benjamin Hawkins was at Fort Mitchell on the Chattahoochee River when he received this intelligence. He was supervising the building of boats and organization of the Creek Indian force that he planned to lead down the river for a joint strike on the outpost. White troops were expected to descend the Flint River under Brigadier General David Blackshear to assist in the operation. While Blackshear would command the campaign, Hawkins would lead his Creek troops. It would be the first time the old soldier of the Revolution had taken the field at the head of large armed force since the close of the Revolutionary War in 1783.

---

[1] Lt. Col. Peter Tooke to Gov. Peter Early, November 21, 1814, Hargrett Rare Book and Manuscript Library, The University of Georgia Libraries, Telamon Cuyler Collection, Box 47, Folder 04, Document 07.

[2] *Ibid.*

[3] *Ibid.*

[4] *Ibid.*

[5] Col. Benjamin Hawkins, "Enrollment of Indians at their several dates up to the 14," Enclosed in Hawkins to Early, November 15, 1814.

[6] Col. Benjamin Hawkins to Gov. Peter Early, November 15, 1814, Hargrett Rare Book and Manuscript Collection, Box 76, Folder 25, Document 28.

[7] Capt. Robert Henry to Admiral Alexander Cochrane, November 22, 1814, Cochrane Papers.

[8] Henry B. Wigginton to Col. Benjamin Hawkins, relaying the report of Capt. Timpoochee Barnard, December 2, 1814.

[9] *Ibid.*

[10] *Ibid.*

[11] Maj. Gen. John McIntosh to Gov. Peter Early, December 12, 1814, Hargrett Rare Book and Manuscript Library, The University of Georgia Libraries, Telamon Cuyler Collection, Box 47, Folder 04, Document 09.

[12] Edward Codrington, letter dated December 14, 1814, in *Memoir of the Life of Admiral Sir Edward Codrington* (Abridged edition), p. 239.

[13] *Ibid.*

[14] *Georgia Journal*, December 21, 1814, p. 5.

[15] Sugden, p. 298.

[16] Report from Milledgeville, Georgia, dated January 11, 1815, published in the Baltimore Patriot on January 30, 1815, p. 3.

[17] *Ibid.*

SIX

British plans to use Nicolls' Outpost as a base for major operations against the Georgia frontier were delayed by the Battle of New Orleans. Lieutenant Colonel Nicolls, the Prophet Francis, Cappachimico, Thomas Perryman and others sailed for Louisiana aboard a Royal Navy warship. Admiral Cochrane and Major General Pakenham expected to overrun Jackson's army with ease and take New Orleans, giving their American Indian guests an impressive view of British military might.

Things did not go as hoped. Pakenham was killed and his army demolished by Andrew Jackson's smaller force, New Orleans remained in American hands and the British were soon withdrawing from the Louisiana coast. The Apalachicola River remained their only foothold on the entire Gulf Coast. Nicolls and the chiefs were soon on their way back to resume their activities there, but quickly found that Colonel Hawkins had not been idle during their absence.

Having shifted his base of operations to Fort Mitchell on the Chattahoochee River in what is now Russell County, Alabama, the U.S. Agent for Indian Affairs undertook the organization of a brigade of Creek warriors from the towns allied with the United States. The largest block of these American Indian soldiers came from Coweta and were led by Major William McIntosh. Also present were Cussetas, Yuchis, Tuckabatchees and others. The loosely organized plan called for Hawkins to lead this force down the Chattahoochee River as a force of Georgia militia and perhaps a few regulars descended the Flint. They would unite near the forks and attack the outpost:

...We also learn that colonel Benjamin Hawkins has upwards of one thousand warriors enrolled in the service of the United States, and to receive soldiers' pay and rations – their head-quarters are at Fort Mitchell, near

[Chattahoochee] River. Col. Hawkins by the request of the warriors have taken the command of them – they say, they can and will fight, and have pledged themselves to do so. These warriors are destined against the Seminoles and hostile Creeks, assembling on the Apalachicolo, a little below the confluence of the Flint and Chattahoochie – a force also of 1600 men composed of mounted men, Choctaws, Chickasaws and Creeks, marched on the 1ˢᵗ inst. from near Tensaw, eastwardly towards Apalatchecola, to co-operate with the exertions of the warriors, headed by colonel Hawkins.[1]

The second column marching from near Tensaw was that of Major Uriah Blue, to which previous reference has been made. Supply shortages and the near starvation of his men prevented Blue from reaching the Apalachicola or forming a junction with Hawkins. Command of the force ordered to the Flint River fell to Brigadier General David Blackshear:

...General Blackshear marched on the 18ᵗʰ inst. with a regiment to Hartford, (Geo.) and from thence to Flint River, which will secure the frontiers of Georgia. It is supposed he will form a junction with colonel Hawkins – this, however, depends on circumstances.[2]

The actual size of Colonel Hawkins' force was around 700 men. They were still gathering at Fort Mitchell to make final arrangements for their campaign as the Battle of New Orleans was fought at Chalmette on January 8, 1815. In fact, it took until early February for Hawkins to assemble enough supplies for his warriors to begin their march down the Chattahoochee River. By February 20, however, they had taken possession of Tockteoethla as Thomas Perryman and his people evacuated their town and fell back to the safety of Nicolls' Outpost. The river was good for boats from Fort Mitchell to that point, Hawkins reported, noting that due to strong counter currents it was possible for a boat to travel from Tocktoethla to Fort Mitchell and back in around 8 days. With an eye to future settlement, the colonel noted that the lands along the east side of the Chattahoochee were of first quality and the banks nearly 50 feet high.[3]

Hawkins and his warriors made camp at Tocktoethla, which he dubbed "115 Mile Camp." The name reflected its distance downstream from Fort Mitchell. Not long after arriving he heard the story of one of the Red Stick leaders that had been present at the Battle of New Orleans. The unidentified chief gave a poignant account of the fighting, noting that the British had been defeated in every battle both day and night. The Americans were so well entrenched, he said, that the British were driven back three times with great losses. The ground was covered with dead and wounded, their commander in chief among them.[4]

The Red Sticks, Hawkins reported to Governor Early, "are very humble." Greater fear was entertained by the agent for "those friendly to us, or who have been Neutral." These Creeks, the colonel noted, were nearly naked and in great distress. The annuity normally paid to the Creek Nation by the United States had been withheld due to the Creek War of 1813-1814. The enemy, Hawkins continued, had plenty of clothing and ammunition.[5]

One of the warriors from Hawkins' command was sent down to Nicolls' Outpost under the guise of being there to receive arms and ammunition. His real mission was to gain intelligence on the fort:

The Hostile force below the forks of the Rivers on the East of the Apalachicolo are about 300 who have entrenched themselves have a breastwork abt. 4 feet high and One Howitzer and one Cohorn. They have 100 whites 80 blacks and the remainder Indians. . . . There is a Spanish officer among them whos rank I know not from Pensacola, and Hugh McGill with some colored people. He ordered a Half breed my informant, who knew him well, out of their fort as being opposed to him and the British.[6]

Hugh McGill was an American deserter from the 2nd U.S. Infantry. He had joined the army at Fort Stoddert, a post at today's Mt. Vernon, Alabama, on April 15, 1812. He was arrested just six weeks later for "Improperly passing the guard &c." Convicted he was sentenced to one week of hard labor. As soon as the week was over, he deserted again. This time McGill got away and fled into Spanish Florida where he joined the British Colonial Marines when Captain Woodbine arrived in Pensacola during the summer of 1814.[7]

The Spanish officer, not otherwise identified, was undoubtedly one of the Cuban soldiers taken aboard the Royal Navy ships from Fort San Carlos de Barrancas when Jackson attacked Pensacola in November 1814. The white soldiers were from the Royal Marines and the black soldiers, since they were not identified by Hawkins as Spanish, were probably from the Colonial Marines battalion being organized by Nicolls and Woodbine.

Colonel Hawkins had expected to join forces at the forks with militia forces from Georgia under Brigadier General David Blackshear. Upon arriving at 115 Mile Camp, however, he heard rumors that Blackshear had turned toward the Atlantic Coast instead. The rumors were true.

General Blackshear had been ordered to the Flint River frontier by Governor Early on December 9, 1814. Similar orders were dispatched from Major General John McIntosh on December 14, instructing Blackshear to march with Wimberly's regiment of Georgia militia to Hartford and from there to open a direct road to the Flint River.[8]

Blackshear made plans to move by ordering Lieutenant Colonel Allen Tooke to secure the tools necessary for building flats on which the infantry could descend the Flint River. Governor Early authorized the use of public tools and sent Captain Thomas' cavalry company to meet the general at the Flint River. These arrangements made, Blackshear ordered Colonel Wimberly to take up the line of march on December 16, 1814.[9]

After Blackshear was on the march, he received a letter from Major General John McIntosh informing him of the arrival of more British warships off the Apalachicola and instructing him to move with all possible speed to meet Colonel Hawkins at the confluence of the Flint and Chattahoochee Rivers. The movement was already underway, but was advancing very slowly. On December 23, for example, Blackshear informed Governor Early that he was delayed at Hartford because he didn't have enough tools to build flats for crossing the Ocmulgee River. He was still there five days later when he notified Early that he had finally gotten part of his command across the river but that supplies and rations were short as the contractor hired to provide them had not appeared. He intended to push forward with or without supplies.[10]

Two days later, however, Blackshear was still at Hartford. He informed General McIntosh on December 30 that he had sent forward pioneers to open a road and build bridges and would march for the Flint on the morning of the 31st. The army had been held up on the Ocmulgee for more than one full week and so far as the general knew, only one day's supply of rations waited ahead.[11]

In Blackshear's defense, the supply situation was desperate and he was being deluged with contradictory orders from General McIntosh and Governor Early due to the flood of intelligence about British activities on the Apalachicola, in Mobile and at New Orleans reaching those individuals. The governor, for example, dispatched orders to Blackshear on January 6, 1815, instructing him to disregard previous instructions to march to the confluence of the Chattahoochee and Flint and move immediately instead for Mobile, Alabama, which General McIntosh believed was threatened by the British. Four days later, however, Early countermanded this new order and instructed Blackshear to continue for the forks. On the 11th, one day after the governor's new orders, McIntosh wrote urging Blackshear on to Mobile.[12]

Additional problems were caused after Blackshear was on the march when the ferry flat at Hartford capsized as a detail was trying to move wagons loaded with supplies across the Ocmulgee. The provisions went to the bottom of the river and further shipments had to be delayed until the flat could be repaired.[13] Throughout all of this, the general's column slowly inched west on its march to the Flint River. The normal rate of march for an infantry column is around 15 miles per day, but Blackshear was moving at a much slower rate. Anticipating the difficulties of moving a large force of white troops on newly cut roads through the wilderness, Colonel Hawkins sent "Coe-e-maut-lau" (Coa Emathla) with written talks for the mestizo chief and trader Jack Kinnard as well as the chiefs at Aummuccalee (today's Muckalee) requesting that they do all in their power to assist the movements of the army.[14]

General Blackshear finally reached the Flint River on January 6, 1815, and immediately set his men to work cutting and hauling timber for the building of a fort. His supply wagons were sent back under escort to bring forward more supplies from Hartford. The fort being built by the troops has often been confused with Fort Early, a nearby work built in 1817 and named in honor of the governor. Blackshear's structure, however, was about one mile north of the later fort and had only reached breastwork level when the barrage of letters instructing him first to Mobile then to the forks of the rivers then to Mobile arrived. He notified General McIntosh on the 14th that he would retrace his route to Hartford and begin a march for Mobile via Fort Hawkins.[15]

Blackshear began his withdrawal from the Flint even as Colonel Hawkins was starting his movement down the Chattahoochee expecting to meet the large militia force at the forks. When Governor Early learned that Blackshear was withdrawing, he made plans to send another 500 white militiamen under Major Freeman to cooperate with Hawkins, but then on January 19 the governor learned of the British landing at Cumberland Island and countermanded all previous orders. General Blackshear was ordered to move to the Georgia coast with all available troops and at all possible speed.[16]

The result of all of this, of course, was that Colonel Hawkins and his 700 Creek warriors were on their own but had no way of knowing it. While Blackshear marched east to Fort Barrington and Darien, Hawkins descended the Chattahoochee to 115 Mile Camp where he sat idly waiting for news from the general. Word of the landing of the British at Cumberland Island had already reached the Creek and Seminole towns and the colonel learned of the rumor from his allies. Recognizing that Blackshear might be recalled to deal with the new threat and that a possible replacement force under General Cark might also be diverted, Hawkins was making plans to go it alone when news reached him that President James Madison had accepted his previously tendered resignation. This left him with no official status so he wrote to Governor Early to explain the situation and request that a man of skill and ability be sent to command. Until someone arrived, he promised to do his best in the situation.[17]

The confusion experienced by civil and military leaders in Georgia in January-February 1815 shows the potential of Nicolls' plan for a strike against the interior of that state. If he had not been diverted to New Orleans, he and Woodbine likely would have hit the frontier just as one British army was battling Jackson at New Orleans and another was coming ashore at Cumberland Island and St. Mary's. The orders that led General Blackshear to withdraw from the Flint and then to proceed to the Atlantic Coast would have come just as the British and Indian force surged north from Nicolls' Outpost. Only Hawkins and his poorly equipped 700 Creeks would have been left to oppose Nicolls, his marines and the well-equipped and now trained Red Sticks and Seminoles. If Hawkins could be defeated, the whole of the interior would have been open to the British just as the force at Cumberland Island was striking along the coast.

The delay occasioned by Nicolls' trip to New Orleans with Cappachimico, Thomas Perryman, the Prophet Francis and others, however, prevented the campaign against the Georgia frontier from ever taking place. Upon his return to the Apalachicola, the British colonel learned of the presence of Hawkins' force north of the forks and – with his stocks of provisions desperately short – went on the defensive. Nicolls went up to the outpost in person with additional troops and warriors. At his request, the Royal Navy also joined in the effort to defend the fort:

...[A]t present...we have eight men in the yawl with a Carronade at the forks of the River Apalachicola (which is the advanced position of our Force, and is situated one hundred and twenty miles from this) to assist in the defence of that Position, which Major Nicolls will have informed you has been threatened with an attack by Colonel Hawkins who is represented to have with him about fifty American Cavalry and nine hundred Indians.[18]

A yawl is a small two-masted sailing vessel, while a carronade is short smoothbore cannon. Since the yawl sent to Nicolls' Outpost was detached from the HMS *Borer*, the carronade likely was one of the ten 18-pounders with which that ship was armed. A crew of eight men was more than capable of maneuvering the boat while also manning the gun, which along with the howitzer and mortar in the outpost gave the British a heavy advantage in artillery over Hawkins' force, which had no cannon.

Colonel Hawkins' second report from 115 Mile Camp shows that Nicolls more than quadrupled the number of warriors at the outpost from 120 to 500 after learning that the American force was nearby:

...Colo. Nicolls with 200 troops white and black and an assemblage of 500 warriors is just below the forks. They have an entrenched post picketed, with one Howitzer and one Cohorn. The Indians are mostly from the Seminoles of East Florida, and Oketeyocanne, Fowltown, and Cheehau within our limits. . . . McQueen and Francis are in uniform. The Col. is gone down today.[19]

Josiah Francis and Peter McQueen were probably wearing the same uniform coats that the British had given them before the Battle of New Orleans. The presence of both of these key Red Stick leaders at the outpost on February 20, 1815, shows that the British were preparing for a major battle against Hawkins and his Creeks. This was further evidenced by the fact that each party of warriors would give their battle cry and paint for war as they reached the British fort.

Hawkins was also preparing for battle, while trying to hold his command together. Many of his Creek soldiers had become disgruntled after General Blackshear's column of Georgia militia failed to appear. They told the colonel that they had been enrolled by order of General Jackson and had been promised the pay and rations of soldiers. They also had been promised that a force of white troops would fight alongside them. No white troops had arrived and they were without meat. In addition, they were displeased to learn that Georgia militia soldiers had garrisoned the frontier forts near which their wives and children lived. These men, they said, were "rude and ungovernable."[20]

Hawkins did not know what to tell his allies so he forwarded their complaint to Governor Early on February 21, 1815. The colonel did not know that he would not be joined by militia, but still thought they were coming just in smaller numbers than originally expected. His location so far south on the international border coupled with the confusion caused by the sudden descent of the British on Cumberland Island, St. Simons Island and St. Mary's literally led to the abandonment of his force in an advanced and exposed position.[21]

Making matters worse, as noted by the chiefs and warriors, the American colonel was having difficulty feeding his men. He had received from Fort

Mitchell a shipment of 90 barrels of flour, 28 bushels of corn and 2 bushels of salt, but only one barrel of pork with which he was expected to feed his more than 700 men for 20 days. He tried sending out detachments to confiscate cattle from nearby villages that had allied with the British, but there was little beef to be had.[22]

Despite such difficulties, Hawkins continued to receive solid intelligence from behind the British lines. This flow of information likely was sustained by sending forward warriors to spy on Nicolls' Outpost under the guise of coming to receive weapons and join the war against the Americans. His spies told him that the Red Sticks beaten by Jackson were humble and that Colonel Nicolls had gone down the river after saying he would be back with supplies to begin a march on Charleston. They would liberate slaves and restore Creek lands as they advanced.[23]

Whatever Colonel Nicolls might have told his allies before heading down the river, however, he knew something that Colonel Hawkins did not. The War of 1812 was over.

[1] *Savannah Republican*, December 22, 1815.

[2] *Ibid.*

[3] Col. Benjamin Hawkins to Gov. Peter Early, February 12, 1815, Hargrett Rare Book and Manuscript Library, The University of Georgia Libraries, Telamon Cuyler Collection, Box 76, Folder 25, Document 20.

[4] Unidentified Red Stick chief to Col. Benjamin Hawkins, quoted in Hawkins to Gov. Peter Early, February 12, 1815, *Ibid.*

[5] Col. Benjamin Hawkins to Gov. Peter Early, February 12, 1815; Col. Benjamin Hawkins to Gov. Peter Early, February 20, 1815, Hargrett Rare Book and Manuscript Library, The University of Georgia Libraries, Telamon Cuyler Collection, Box 77, Folder 25, Document 21.

[6] Col. Benjamin Hawkins to Gov. Peter Early, February 12, 1815, quoted in Mark F. Boyd, "Historic Sites in and around the Jim Woodruff Reservoir Area, Florida-Georgia," River Basin Surveys Papers, No 13, *Bulletin 169*, Smithsonian Institution, Bureau of American Ethnology, 1958, p 270.

[7] Registers of Enlistments in the United States Army, 1798-1914, Volume M-0, 1798-May 17, 1815, NARA M233, Roll Number 9, p. 179.

[8] Gov. Peter Early to Brig. Gen. David Blackshear, December 9, 1814, copy in author's collection; Maj. Gen. John McIntosh to Gen. David Blackshear, December 14, 1814, copy in author's collection.

[9] Brig. Gen. David Blackshear to Lt. Col. Allen Tooke, December 12, 1814, copy in author's collection; Gov. Peter Early to Brig. Gen. David Blackshear, December 14 & 16,

1814, copies in author's collection; Brig. Gen. David Blackshear to Col. Wimberly and Major Lawson, December 16, 1814, copy in author's collection
[10] Maj. Gen. John McIntosh to Brig. Gen. David Blackshear, December 19, 1814, copy in author's collection; Brig. Gen. David Blackshear to Gov. Peter Early, December 23, 1814, copy in author's collection; Brig. Gen. David Blackshear to Gov. Peter Early, December 28, 1814, copy in author's collection.
[11] Brig. Gen. David Blackshear to Maj. Gen. John McIntosh, December 30, 1814, copy in author's collection.
[12] Gov. Peter Early to Brig, Gen. David Backshear, January 6, 1815, copy in author's collection; Gov. Peter Early to Brig. Gen. David Blackshear, January 10, 1815, copy in author's collection; Maj. Gen. John McIntosh to Brig. Gen. David Blackshear, January 11, 1815, copy in author's collection.
[13] A. McDonald to Brig. Gen. David Blackshear, January 3, 1815, copy in author's collection.
[14] Col. Benjamin Hawkins to Jack Kennard, January 11, 1814, and Col. Benjamin Hawkins to chiefs of Am-mic-cul-le, January 11, 1814, copies in author's collections.
[15] Brig. Gen. David Blackshear to Maj. Gen. John McIntosh, January 11 & January 14, 1815, copies in author's collection.
[16] Gov. Peter Early to Brig. Gen. David Blackshear, January 16 & 19, 1815, copies in author's collection.
[17] Col. Benjamin Hawkins to Gov. Peter Early, February 12, 1815.
[18] Capt. William Rawlins to Admiral Percy Malcolm, February 26, 1815, Cochrane Papers (Sent from HMS *Borer*, "St. George's Sound").
[19] Col. Benjamin Hawkins to Gov. Peter Early, February 20, 1815, quoted by Mark F. Boyd, "Historic Sites in and around the Jim Woodruff Reservoir Area, Florida-Georgia."
[20] Statement of U.S. Creek allies, quoted in postscript dated February 21, 1815, Col. Benjamin Hawkins to Gov. Peter Early, February 20, 1815.
[21] *Ibid.*
[22] *Ibid.*; Col. Benjamin Hawkins to Gov. Peter Early, February 24, 1815, Hargrett Rare Book and Manuscript Library, The University of Georgia Libraries, Telamon Cuyler Collection, Box 76, Folder 25, Document 22.
[23] Col. Benjamin Hawkins to Gov. Peter Early, February 24, 1815.

SEVEN

The reason that Colonel Nicolls left the outpost with an American force immediately before him was revealed in a letter that he sent to Rear Admiral Percy Malcolm. He explained to the admiral that he had "returned by water" from his "advanced post" after learning that Captain Irby of the HMS *Thames* had arrived off Apalachicola Bay with critical news:

I have the honor to acquaint you that I have received from Captain Irby of the Thames, Letters from the Commander in Chief acquainting me of a Treaty of Peace being signed by the Commissioners of the United States and those of England which has been ratified by the Prince Regent that when it receives the ratification of the President of the United States is to be considered final, and all hostilities to cease, also directing me to act on the defensive only until such ratification takes place and t recommend the same to the Indians; all of which I have complied with.[1]

The distance between the two British forts was around 80 miles, but by water via the twisting and turning channel of the Apalachicola it was nearly twice that far. It took a full week for Colonel Nicolls to go down to Prospect Bluff and the bay and then for his dispatch to subordinate officers to make it back up to the outpost. In the meantime his forces continued to prepare for battle, as did those of Colonel Hawkins. The American commander was trying to block the departure of any raiding parties from the outpost while also contemplating his next move. He moved his camp about one mile from its original position at Tocktoethla in order to find better cane for the horses. Most of the enemy warriors, he reported, had withdrawn back below the Florida line although a couple of small war parties were still out. If the British advanced, he expected fighting. Otherwise, he planned to remain on the defensive.[2]

Hawkins appears to have underestimated the strength and intent of the war parties being sent against the Georgia frontier by the British at Nicolls Outpost. Col. Nicolls expressed concern about them in his letter to Admiral Malcolm:

...I fear that sad mischief will be done by parties I have detached, before news can reach them – within the last three weeks the Indians have done considerable damage to the people of the Frontiers, and nothing but the want of Provisions had prevented me from joining you with 2,000 men. Our advanced post is 80 miles from hence [i.e. Prospect Bluff] from which I returned by water the day Captain Irby arrived, by the latter Conveyance it is 170 miles.[3]

Still unaware of the signing of the Treaty of Ghent, Hawkins contemplated a move on the Seminole town of Miccosukee where he knew that his men could find plenty of beef. He informed Governor Early that barring the receipt of new information from the governor by February 27, he would act on "my own views as will best secure your frontiers during the sojourn of the enemy on your sea coast." He reported rumors that the Spanish governor in Pensacola had sent an armed vessel to retrieve "McGill and the Spanish negroes." And although he had not met Colonel Nicolls, he called him "quite the blustering braggadocio."[4]

Neither Hawkins nor Nicolls knew it, but as the former officer was writing his letter to Governor Early at 115 Mile Camp on February 24, 1815, the last land battle of the War of 1812 was taking place some 200 miles to the east on the St. Mary's River. Planning to destroy a sawmill near today's Folkston, Georgia, a boat party of British marines, sailors and officers had gone up the St. Mary's. They ran into a buzz saw of fire from both sides of the river as U.S. riflemen and Florida revolutionaries calling themselves "Patriots" rushed to the attack:

... [T]hough attacked upon both sides, and in a river but from 30 to 50 yards wide in most parts of it, the flotilla fought its way through. Our loss on the occasion was but 29 in killed and wounded, of the latter eighteen severely – Capt. Phaliot, early in the action, received a buckshot above the left knee, and a flesh wound in the right thigh: capt. Bartholomew was struck in five different parts of the body, but, though severely wounded, continued in the discharge of his duty, nor would he allow himself to be dressed until every individual wounded was done before him.[5]

The British were driven back without achieving their objective and while they downplayed their 29 killed and wounded, the Americans reported only one man wounded in the battle. It was the last time that land forces of the United States and Great Britain would ever face each other in battle.

On the day after the Battle of the St. Mary's, a courier arrived at 115 Mile Camp bringing Colonel Hawkins news of the end of the war from his assistant, Christian Limbaugh. The courier carried a copy of the announcement of the Postmaster General of the United States that a peace treaty had been received. The colonel immediately sent two runners to take the information to the British officer in command at Nicolls' Outpost, but they were met by a flag of truce coming from the fort with the same news. The flag was born by two lieutenants, one from the navy and one from the army.[6]

The news of peace instantly turned bitter enemies into friends. Colonel Hawkins welcomed the two British lieutenants to enjoy the hospitality of his camp. Although he did not identify them, one may have been either Lieutenant Samuel Smith or Lieutenant James Denney of the Royal Marines. Both had been on the Apalachicola River since May 1814. They remained with the colonel at 115 Mile Camp on the night of February 25, 1815, and returned to the outpost the next day. A *feu de joie* was fired on the evening of the 25th and another on the morning of the 26th as the British officers reviewed a parade of Hawkins' men.[7]

A *feu de joie* is a unique military salute that translates from the original French to literally mean a "fire of joy." Sometimes called a "running fire," it involves a line of soldiers firing one after another into the air in quick succession. When done at night, a *feu de joie* literally creates the appearance of a rippling line of fire that extends from one end of a formation to the other. The firing of one is a moment of great ceremony and they are only done to celebrate landmark moments in national history. In the United States, for example, one was fired in 1778 at Valley Forge to celebrate the arrival of news that France was entering the American Revolution on the side of the Patriots. Himself a soldier of the Revolution, Colonel Hawkins undoubtedly remembered this use of the salute and recognized that the end of the War of 1812 was a moment of equal importance.

The salute was followed by dinner at which Hawkins and his officers sat down with their guests to enjoy a meal and conversations. In the matter of a moment, the men had gone from being enemies to friends and those from each side appear to have welcomed the companionship of the other. The next morning, after the firing of the second *feu de joie* and the review of Hawkins' command by the British officers, they returned to Nicolls' Outpost as he gave orders to his Creek allies to prepare for their return march home.[8]

The British had arrived at 115 Mile Camp bearing only the 9th article of the Treaty of Ghent, but it was one that was of vital importance to their Red Stick allies:

> *The United States of America engage to put an end immediately after the Ratification of the present Treaty to hostilities with all the Tribes or Nations of Indians with whom they may be at war at the time of such Ratification, and forthwith to restore such Tribes or Nations respectively all the possessions, rights, and privileges which they may have enjoyed or been entitled to in one thousand eight hundred and eleven previous to such hostilities....[9]*

The 9th article of the treaty went on to require each side to prevent their American Indian allies from attacking the other and to always remain at peace. For the Red Stick Creeks, and indeed for the U.S. allied Creeks as well, the requirement that the United States return all "property" back to the Indians had enormous implications. Andrew Jackson had signed the Treaty of Fort Jackson with a delegation of Creek chiefs on August 9, 1814. The signing of the document, an act to which the Red Sticks in Florida had not been invited to participate, stripped the Creek Nation of more than 23 million acres of land.

Under the British interpretation of the 9th article, the "property" to be restored to the Creeks included the 23 million acres taken from then by the Treaty of Fort Jackson. The United States did not agree. In the view of the Americans, the Creek War of 1813-1814 was a separate war from the War of 1812 and the treaty concluded at Fort Jackson had nothing to do with the British or the Treaty of Ghent. This dispute would lead to more difficulty between the United States and Great Britain over the British forts on the Apalachicola River.

Hawkins and his men began to evacuate 115 Mile Camp on February 26, 1815. Dividing the warriors into multiple columns, the colonel ordered them home via different routes, both as a means of alleviating the chronic food shortage and to spread the word to all of the Creek villages they encountered that a peace treaty had been signed. Colonel Nicolls also set about bringing the war to an end, but using very different methods:

> *...The Indians who first engaged in the War are in a most wretched state, and I hope Provisions will be sent to me for them soon, with the last supply I*

got we have no only three weeks for our own people and we are obliged to victual several Indians who are necessary to our movements; in ten days from this I am to have a general meeting of the Chiefs at our Fort on the Forks of the Chatahouche and Flint Rivers, to the collectively I shall communicate the terms of Peace, but for the individuals to whom I have already communicated it they have replied that unless they have free communication with us and a British officer kept with them they are sure of destruction.[10]

The date for the council of chiefs at the outpost was set for March 10. In the same report, however, Nicolls also indicated that he expected to evacuate the outpost soon after that date. "As soon as I hear from the American Colonel commanding opposite to me that the Treaty is accepted," he wrote, "I shall cause my advance to retire to this post [i.e. Prospect Bluff]." He also noted that he had reported to his Red Stick and Seminole allies "the order of the Admiral about leaving them plenty of arms, ammunition &c., and even cannon, with which they are well pleased." The chiefs emphasized to him, however, that the "presence of a British officer is indispensable."[11]

Nicolls recognized that the request of his allies for a British officer to be placed in control of their affairs in Florida would be an affront to Spain, a dying empire yet one that still held legal possession of the colony. He warned Rear Admiral Malcolm, however, that the Indians were prepared to attack the Spanish if they were not granted their request:

...I have told them that if it is the will of my Government, I will remain and see justice done to them with pleasure, they are very much exasperated against the Spaniards, and it is as much as I can do to prevent them from driving the Garrison of St. Marks, and indeed all the other Garrisons out of the Province. They positively declare that if Spain does not suffer them a free communication through the Appalachicola river between them and the British they will declare war without quarter against her Subjects. I think it would be good policy in our Government to demand from Spain such terms, for unless that is the case we can never get to the Indians to supply them with powder, arms & c....[12]

Always the military man, Colonel Nicolls was anticipating wars of the future when he wrote that "we may always calculate on their assisting us either against Spain or America." Considering the history of his lifetime, he could not have imagined that Great Britain and the United States were even then embarking on 200 years of friendship.

The Americans evacuated 115 Mile Camp by the end of February 1815, but the British continued to hold both of their forts on the Apalachicola. High ranking British officers, Nicolls among them, continued their efforts to restrain their Red Stick allies from further attacks on the United States, especially after learning of the formal ratification of the Treaty of Ghent. Rear Admiral George Cockburn learned of the ratification on March 10, 1815, and sent a call for an end to hostilities to "the Chief of any Indian tribe on or near the border of Georgia." His written letter was dispatched to Colonel Nicolls both through American officers and as an enclosure in a dispatch from Rear Admiral Malcolm.[13]

The future of the Red Stick Creeks and Seminoles was the entire focus when the chiefs and principal warriors gathered by the upper Apalachicola on March 10, 1815. The Creeks had been dealing with the British in one way or another since 1674. The council at Nicolls' Outpost, however, would mark the last time a treaty would ever be signed between the two groups. In fact, the document produced by Colonel Nicolls and the chiefs is believed to be last agreement ever concluded between the British and American Indians in what is now the United States east of the Mississippi River.

The number of chiefs and warriors that appeared for the council was large. Among the key American Indian leaders present were Cappachimico, Thomas Perryman, the Prophet Francis, Peter McQueen, Homathlemico and three men named Eneah Emathla (Neamathla). One of these was the Fowltown chief who would achieve note for his defiance of U.S. expansionism during the years 1817-1836. Among the items found when his home was raided by U.S. troops in 1817 were a British uniform coat with epaulets and a letter signed by an officer affirming that the chief had always been a true friend of the British.

In addition to seeking the continued support of Great Britain, the chiefs took retaliatory action against John Forbes & Company by rescinding the so-called Forbes Purchase. Actually two major land cessions, the purchase had been exacted from the Lower Creeks and Seminoles prior to the War of 1812 in lieu of payment in cash of debts owed by the Indians to the trading company. Colonel Nicolls considered cancellation of the Forbes Purchase to be a matter of great importance:

...They have by a public act in full assembly confiscated the lands given to and all the property of the house of Forbes & Co. for breach of contract with them and for endeavouring to prevent them from joining us – Indeed I know this

to be true for I have intercepted letters from [John] Forbes at St. Augustine and from [James] Innerarity the Mayor of Mobille which if they are to be considered as British will shew them to be guilty of Treason, and I personally know the partner of the house at Pensacola [i.e. John Innerarity] to be the greatest rascal on earth, one who has abused the British in the grossest terms, and praised the Americans in the strongest manner, of which I have seen written proofs by his own hand.[14]

The Innerarity brothers, mentioned in Nicolls' report to Rear Admiral Percy Malcolm, were nephews of William Panton, one of the original partners in the Panton, Leslie & Company trading firm. The company later became John Forbes & Company, in which both James and John Innerarity were partners. John Forbes headed the company's facilities in St. Augustine while John Innerarity headed its establishment in Pensacola. James Innerarity lived in Pensacola, which had been a Spanish city until it was seized by the United States in 1813. He was elected First President of Commissioners (Mayor) the following year. The two Innerarity brothers were associates of Andrew Jackson and, as Nicolls correctly deduced, opposed the British during the War of 1812.
Little is known of the discussions at the council, which was also attended by Colonel Nicolls, Captain Henry Ross of the British Rifle Corps, Captain Joseph Roche of the 1st West India Regiment and Lieutenant William Hambly, the former and future Forbes & Company employee who served as interpreter. The document that resulted from the talks still survives, however, and was addressed to King George III by the 30 chiefs present at the Outpost. In it they pleaded with the King to maintain open ports for them at the mouths of the Apalachicola, Alabama and St. Mary's Rivers:

...[F]or if our communication is once more cut off from his children, we shall be totally ruined; we have fought and bled for him against the Americans, by which we have made them our more bitter enemies, and as he has stood the friend of oppressed nation beyond the great waters, he will surely not forget the sufferings of his once happy children here. We therefore rely on his future protection and his fatherly kindness: we will truly keep the talks which his chief has given us, if he is graciously pleased to continue his protection....[15]

As they continued to explain their situation to the King, the chiefs revealed just how desperate the formerly prosperous Seminoles had become, despite assistance from the British for which they were grateful:

...[F]amine is now devouring up ourselves and our children, by reason of our Upper Town brethren being driven down upon us in the time the corn was green, and now their miseries and necessities cause them to root up the seed of our future crop, so that we sow in the day we are obliged to watch at night. Was it not for the powder we get from your chief, the whole of the nation would be in dust: the Red Sticks have shot and eat up almost the whole of our cattle, for they have seen their children digging in the woods for want, and who can blame them, when they are pressed by such cruel necessity? Thus are we situated, and are only looking to the departure or the stay of your children, as the signal of our destruction or prosperity.[16]

As the Prophet Francis was among the signers of the Nicolls' Outpost document, the starving children referenced included his own son and daughters. One of these, Milly, would become one of the most remarkable women in American history. Three years later she saved the life of a Georgia militiaman named Duncan McCrimmon and became known as the Creek Pocahontas. In 1815, however, she was around 12 years old and was living in destitution with her family on the Apalachicola River.[*]

The chiefs went on to explain that they had made land grants to both Panton, Leslie & Company and John Forbes & Company, but the companies had failed to keep their promises to settle the lands with "British men" and maintain good supplies of merchandise for Indian use:

...[I]nstead of their doing this, they have attempted to settle our lands with Americans, and have refused to supply us with powder, when we were attacked by our enemies, and have urges us to declare for the Americans against the British, and have offered rewards to us for that purpose; and they have actually written to their agents who reside among us, desiring them to obstruct the British officers all in their power from assisting us, and to represent to them, alas, how impossible it would be for them to succeed against the Americans....[17]

The agents were Edmund Doyle and William Hambly, the two company employees that had operated the trading post at Prospect Bluff prior to the arrival of the British. Letters to them had been intercepted by Creek and Seminole warriors, in retaliation for which the chiefs told the King that they

---

[*] For more on her life, please see *Milly Francis: The Life & Times of the Creek Pocahontas* by this author.

were rescinding their agreement with the Forbes company. "We further annul and declare void our grant or grants of land accordingly," the document continued, "warning them and all belonging to them to never appear again in the nation."[18]

The chiefs next explained that they had objected to and been harmed by the running of the Old Federal Road through the Creek Nation. It linked Hartford, Georgia, to Fort Stoddert near Mobile, Alabama. They had sent William McIntosh of Coweta, who they termed a "young chief" and who was now their enemy, to protest against the running of the road but instead he had betrayed them. According to their allegation, McIntosh had been "tricked by the enemy" and unlawfully sold Creek lands on the Oconee and Ocmulgee Rivers. They asked for the king's help in ending American use of the Federal Road and in having the Oconee and Ocmulgee lands restored to them:

...The above-mentioned McIntosh holds a commission as Major in the American army, and the Creek Regiment: he has caused much blood to be spilt, for which we denounce him to the whole nation, and will give the usual reward of the brave who may kill him, he having on a recent occasion killed and scalped a brother who was on an errand of peace to our Cherokee brethren, for no other reason alleged against him than his having British arms about him, and in this we are told he has been encouraged by Colonel Hawkins, although long after a peace was declared, and all hostility ordered to cease.[19]

The chiefs concluded by asking that Colonel Nicolls "return our grateful thanks to our good Father and his chiefs." They also thanked the colonel and his officers for "their brotherly conduct to us." In expression of their gratitude to the British for respecting their lands in the Treaty of Ghent, they declared that they would consider as an enemy anyone who would try to sell any of their lands:

...[W]e do further declare, that whosoever shall endeavour directly or indirectly to separate us from him [i.e. King George], or his children, to be the enemy of us and our children, and that we will not trade or barter with any other than the British nation, if the above requests be complied with and we do promise to give grants of land to all such British men as our good Gather shall give permission to stay among us, and that we will do our best to protect and defend them in their laws and property: and we send as our representative, our

brave brother Hidlis Hadgo (Francis) to our good Father, who is authorized to ratify this treaty.[20]

The remarkable document was marked by the 30 chiefs and witnessed by Nicolls, Ross, Roche and Hambly. Its concluding line notes that it was "given under our hands at the British Fort, at the confluence of the Chatutouchee and Flint rivers, this 10th March, 1815." The signers included Red Sticks, Lower Creeks, Seminoles, Miccosukees and Alachuas. It was the final agreement ever negotiated between representatives of Great Britain and the American Indians of the eastern United States. More importantly, it marked the formalization of an alliance among the Indian groups themselves. The little known Nicolls' Outpost treaty completed the formation of what would thereafter be known as the Seminole Nation of Florida.

---

[1] Lt. Col. Edward Nicolls to Rear Admiral Percy Malcolm, February-March 1815, Cochrane Papers.
[2] Col. Benjamin Hawkins to Gov. Peter Early, February 24, 1815.
[3] Lt. Col. Edward Nicolls to Rear Admiral Percy Malcom, February-March 1815.
[4] Col. Benjamin Hawkins to Gov. Peter Early, February 24, 1815.
[5] Report from Halifax, Nova Scotia, dated March 29, 1815, published by the Lexington, Kentucky, *Reporter*, May 10, 1815, p. 3.
[6] Col. Benjamin Hawkins to Gov. Peter Early, February 26, 1815, Hargrett Rare Book and Manuscript Library, The University of Georgia Libraries, Telamon Cuyler Collection, Box 76, Folder 25, Document 23.
[7] *Ibid.*
[8] *Ibid.*
[9] Treaty of Ghent, Article the Ninth, December 24, 1814.
[10] Lt. Col. Edward Nicolls to Rear Admiral Percy Malcolm, February-March 1815.
[11] *Ibid.*
[12] *Ibid.*
[13] Rear Admiral George Cockburn to the Chief of any Indian tribe on or near the Border of Georgia, March 10, 1815, Hargrett Rare Book and Manuscript Library, The University of Georgia Libraries, Telamon Cuyler Collection, Box 82, Folder 18, Document 01 (signed aboard the HMS *Albion* off Cumberland Island).
[14] Lt. Col. Edward Nicolls to Rear Admiral Percy Malcolm, February-March 1815.
[15] Address of the Indians to the King of England, on the Conclusion of the Treaty of Peace, March 10, 1815, *The London Times*, August 13, 1818.
[16] *Ibid.*
[17] *Ibid.*
[18] *Ibid.*
[19] *Ibid.*
[20] *Ibid.*

EIGHT

The council of March 10 was the last known event of significance at Nicolls' Outpost, but the British continued to hold the fort for several more weeks. Several war parties from Fowltown were still out, having been dispatched to strike the Georgia frontier before news of the peace treaty had arrived two weeks earlier. William Hardridge, an emissary sent by Colonel Hawkins to Prospect Bluff as the American force was preparing to withdraw from 115 Mile Camp, reached that post on February 26, 1815. He met there with Captain Ross of the Rifle Corps who told him that Colonel Nicolls had gone to meet with the admirals on the Gulf of Mexico.[1]

According to a report written by Hawkins two months later, Hardridge's primary mission was to meet with Nicolls about the return of slaves that had fled from farms along the Georgia frontier – including the one owned by Hawkins at the Creek Agency. Ross told him that he had no instructions from Nicolls and could do nothing until that officer returned. Curiously, Hawkins' report notes that some of the black recruits at Prospect Bluff had "run away from the negroes and white people." This implies at least that some of the former slaves at the British post had been owned by other people of color.[2]

Hardridge reported that provisions were in very short supply at the bluff and that the Creek and Seminole families were living on alligators. One woman, he was told, had eaten her own child. Captain Ross asked the emissary if the United States had withdrawn all of its troops from the Creek Nation. When Hardridge told him that the soldiers remained at their posts in Creek country, the captain explained to him the British position that they alone were to protect the Creeks in the future.[3]

The American representative remained at the bluff for only three days, during which time he examined the fort there and saw around 500 Creeks and Seminoles inside the defenses. Whether this number included women and children or listed warriors alone is not known. The British by this time had assembled more than 2,500 American Indian allies on the Apalachicola, but hundreds of warriors were upriver at the outpost and others were in the woods trying to find game with which to feed their families.

Hardridge had left Prospect Bluff on his return to Georgia by the time Colonel Nicolls made his way back up the river. The council at Nicolls' Outpost followed on March 10 and then began a long waiting game in which the British clearly expected the United States to restore to the Creeks the lands ceded at the Treaty of Fort Jackson. It never happened. American authorities considered the Creek War of 1813-1814 to have been unconnected to the larger War of 1812. It was already over by the time the British arrived on the Gulf Coast and, in the minds of U.S. officials, the Treaty of Fort Jackson had nothing to do with the Treaty of Ghent.

Colonel Nicolls, believing that he might be ordered to remain behind as the British agent to the Creeks and Seminoles, recognized that the Apalachicola River would be a lonely and dangerous place for an Irishman far from home once the troops were withdrawn:

...If I am left here after the forces are withdrawn, I hope you will be so good as to let me have one or two officers of my choice and some non commissioned officers & a few Privates, as it is a wild Country to travel through even in Peace – and I also request you will e so good as to let Captain Rawlins of the Borer remain with me if a vessel of war is to be left, - We also want two small Schooners that belonged to this place and are now with you [i.e. Rear Admiral Percy Malcolm], and if you can spare us any other that does not draw more than 6 feet she will be of great service to us.[4]

As the process of evacuating the forts on the Apalachicola stalled, the Americans and Spanish grew more concerned. Governor Mateo Gonzales Manrique in Pensacola was under considerable pressure from John Innerarity and other residents of his city to secure the return of their slaves from the Apalachicola River. The British had finally carried 70 of the Cuban troops from Fort Barrancas back, but others still remained on the river as did numbers of now liberated slaves from Pensacola. At least some of the Spanish soldiers were still at Nicolls' Outpost in March 1815. A large group of Pensacola residents petitioned the governor for his help:

...[I]t is public and notorious that all our slaves were seduced with deceptions and carried off by force in such a way as may be supposed on account of the benefit that would result to Nicolls by the formation of his Colonial Regiment, by which he would obtain the confirmation of his Colonelcy, and it is known that even the Indians have suffered equal oppressions from Captn. Woodbine and his other Agents, who despoiled them of their slaves, whom they keep in the Fort they have built on the River Appalachicola.[5]

The same situation existed in St. Augustine, where Captain Woodbine had encouraged slaves to leave the farms and plantations surrounding the old city and join the Colonial Marines. Governor Sebastian Kindelan ordered Woodbine out of the city and province but the losses sustained by Spanish citizens were large. Because he had no direct communication with the English in the Gulf, Governor Kindelan appealed to his counterpart in Pensacola for help. Governor Manrique forwarded Kindelan's request to Captain R.C. Spencer of the Royal Navy: The governor appealed to Captain R.C. Spencer of the Royal Navy for help in restoring the losses inflicted by Captain Woodbine:

...[U]pon his return he took away a number of Slaves & horses belonging to different inhabitants and planters of this Province, entrusted to my care, and consider it my duty to claim them for their account and also of the Chua [i.e. Alachua] Indians protected by this Government which the said English Officer had also taken away and encorporated with his detachment. I conceive it incumbent on me to use every exertion in furthering their views and supposing you to have more immediate intercourse with the British Commanders I request you to represent to them in the name of the Spanish Government to that effect....[6]

Governor Manrique also appealed directly to the British commanders in the Gulf, outlining the case of both the Spanish government and the citizens of Florida for the return of their former slaves. The former slaves, however, were now members of the British military and had been promised their freedom in exchange for enlisting. They would not be returned.

As March continued, Colonel Nicolls did begin to scale back his force at the Outpost. The artillery was removed from the fort and carried back to Prospect Bluff, where the main British force was concentrating ahead of its expected withdrawal from Florida. Most of the troops also went back down the river and by April only a small detachment was still in place at the outpost. When Captain Vicente Sebastian Pintado arrived at Prospect Bluff from Pensacola to bring back any slaves that would like to return as well as any remaining Spanish troops still in British hands, Nicolls told him that the fort near the forks was an earthen redoubt ("redoubt of land") garrisoned by just a handful of men. If Pintado desired it, the colonel said, he would order the post abandoned and destroyed. The post at Prospect Bluff, however, would be left in the hands of the Indians and black Colonial Marines.[7]

Pintado's report, dated April 29, 1815, was the last official mention of a British force still in place at the forks. Nicolls' Outpost was evacuated shortly after the Spanish officer left the Apalachicola River. The exact date of the abandonment of the fort is not known.

The British remained on the river until May 14, 1815, when they finally left Prospect Bluff. The extensive fort there and an impressive armament of cannon, powder and small arms was left in the hands of the locally-raised men of the Colonial Marines along with the Red Sticks, Seminoles and a small party of around 30 Choctaw warriors. Lieutenant William Hambly, the former John Forbes & Company employee was left in command. Recognizing that the British likely would not be back, however, he left the fort within a few months and returned to his former occupation with the trading company. Command of the fort then fell to the sergeant major of the company, a 30-year-old former carpenter from Pensacola named Garcon or Garzon. He shared his responsibilities with two other former carpenters, Cyrus and Prince. The black troops continued to wear their uniforms, conduct drills and fly the British flag over the bluff.[8]

The Prophet Josiah Francis accepted the commission given to him at the Nicolls' Outpost council to represent the Red Sticks and Seminoles before King George. He and his son Earle left the Apalachicola River with Colonel Nicolls, boarding the brig HMS *Forward* for the trip around Florida and up the east coast to the mouth of the St. Mary's River. They reached Amelia Island on June 7, 1815:

It is proper your Excellency should know, that on the 7th instant a brig and transport arrived at Amelia Island, with Col. Nicolls, Capt. Woodbine, an Indian chief and his son. They have been asked if they were prepared to take possession of the Province? One of them replied, they were not yet supplied with money and provisions for the purpose – that it was the sole cause of the delay; the supply was soon expected.[9]

The alleged response about a plan to take possession of Spanish East Florida was not sincere. The British had no plans to seize the colony. The stop at Amelia Island was simply to take on board water and provisions. An American citizen of Fernandina wrote on June 10 that "Lieut. Col. Nichol and Capt. Woodbine, with an Indian Chief, were on board – also, about 50 Negro troops."[10]

The *Forward* was still off Amelia Island as late as June 14, 1815, but she finally set sail and reached Murray's Anchorage at Bermuda on June 27, 1815. Two days later she set sail for Great Britain with the colonel and the prophet aboard. The ship reached England after a fast sail and Nicolls arrived in London on August 14, 1815. Francis and his son were given rooms at the colonel's home, Durham Lodge, in Kent. Any hope the officer might have had for a favorable response from his government was quickly dashed. Although he requested a meeting with Earl Bathurst to discuss the situation of the Creeks and Seminoles, Nicolls received no response other than instructions that Francis be given a set of presentation pistols.[11]

Although Francis was finally presented to the Prince Regent, the British had no interest in ratifying the Nicolls' Outpost Treaty and risking a new war with the Americans. The Creeks and Seminoles had been their allies, but the will to risk war in order to help them was no longer there. The Prophet was disappointed by this and by the unwillingness of his friends to help restore the lands they had promised that his people would receive under the 9th section of the Treaty of Ghent. His anger with the Americans, however, remained great. "He swears he will kill every American in the province as soon as he returns," Nicolls wrote of Francis on December 19, 1815.[12]

The rejection by British leaders of the treaty negotiated by Colonel Nicolls was the last official act associated with Nicolls' Outpost. The Prophet left England to return home on December 30, 1816. By that time American gunboats had destroyed the fort at Prospect Bluff, killing 270 of the 320 or so men, women and children within its walls. The "hot shot" fired by the U.S. Navy into the powder magazine of the fort was the deadliest cannon shot in American history.

The earthen walls of Nicolls' Outpost remained visible for many years, although the British probably burned the wooden parts of the fort when they abandoned it in April 1815. U.S. reports on the First Seminole War battle remembered today as the Scott Massacre note that the action took place at "Fort

Apalachicola," the name sometimes given by American authorities to the outpost. The site of the fort overlooks the scene where Red Stick, Seminole and Black Seminole warriors attacked an army boat and killed 34 men, 6 women and 4 children on November 30, 1817.[*]

Others noted the fading traces of the earthworks over the years and the "old fort" continued to be shown on maps of Florida for several decades. The Comte de Castelnau, a French nobleman that explored Florida during the 1830s, noted that he had seen trenches, "evidently modern," atop one of the tumuli or mounds at today's River Landing Park in Chattahoochee. An old soldier told him that they dated from the time of Andrew Jackson's invasion of Florida.

Time and the elements finally wiped away the last vestiges of the fort and no visible sign of it remains today. The site is protected today, but artifact hunters of earlier generations found reminders of the British presence in the form of musketballs, buttons and more. One of the buttons, a sleeve button from an officer of the Royal Marines, was of a type used by officers of the rank of major or above. The only officer of that grade at Nicolls' Outpost during the time of its military importance was Colonel Nicolls himself.

Chattahoochee Main Street, the City of Chattahoochee, and the West Gadsden Historical Society placed a historical marker at the site in November 2014 as part of an event commemorating the 200th anniversary of the building of the fort. The site marks the northernmost reach of the 1814-1815 British campaign on the Gulf Coast.

---

[1] Col. Benjamin Hawkins to Gov. Peter Early, April 24, 1815, Hargrett Rare Book and Manuscript Library, The University of Georgia Libraries, Telamon Cuyler Collection, Box 76, Folder 25, Document 24.

[2] *Ibid.*

[3] *Ibid.*

[4] Lt. Col. Edward Nicolls to Rear Admiral Percy Malcolm, February-March 1815.

[5] John Forbes & Co. *et. al.* to Gov. Mateo Gonzales Manrique, March 1815, Cochrane Papers.

[6] Gov. Sebastian Kindelan to Gov. Mateo Gonzales Manrique, quoted in Gov. Mateo Gonzales Manrique to Capt. R.C. Spencer, March 11, 1815, Cochrane Papers.

[7] Vicente Sebastian Pintado to Jose de Soto, April 29, 1815, Pintado Papers.

---

[*] For a detailed account of this battle, please see *The Scott Massacre of 1817* by this author.

---

[8] Claudio Saunt, *A New Order of Things: Property, Power, and the Transformation of the Creek Indians, 1733-1816*, Cambridge University Press, New York, pp 282-283.

[9] Gentleman in St. Mary's to Gov. Peter Early, June 10, 1815, published in the *Georgia Journal* on June 21, 1815.

[10] Gentleman in Fernandina to a friend in Savannah, June 10, 1815, published in the *Savannah Museum* on June 15, 1815.

[11] Sugden, p. 308.

[12] Lt. Col. Edward Nicolls, December 19, 1815, Cochrane Papers.

NINE

A remarkable number of individuals prominent in the history of North America were associated with the history of Nicolls' Outpost. This chapter examines the later lives of some of the more prominent.

General Sir Edward Nicolls, K.C.B.

Lieutenant Colonel Nicolls would go on to serve some 40 years in the Royal Marines, eventually rising to the rank of general and being awarded the title of Knight Commander of the Order of the Bath. Often called "Fighting Nicolls," he took part in more than 100 engagements on behalf of his king of country and was wounded many times. After leaving Florida, where he held the temporary rank of lieutenant colonel, he returned to the rank of captain and brevet major. He hosted the Prophet Francis and his son, Earle, at his home in England until the end of 1815 but failed in his effort to have Francis recognized as a formal ambassador from the Creeks. When the prophet left to return home, his son remained behind with Nicolls who saw to his education.

Nicolls was named commandant of Ascension Island in 1823. The small volcanic island is in the South Atlantic roughly 1,000 miles from Africa and 1,400 miles from South America. It was seized by Great Britain in 1815 to prevent its use as a base by French interests that might try to liberate Napoleon Bonaparte from his exile on Saint Helena. Because it was against British law for the Royal Navy to govern a colony, Ascension was officially considered a small ship by Great Britain. Brevet Major Nicolls is remembered there for building pipelines that brought water to settled areas from springs in the island's mountains.

Nicolls was promoted to the full rank of major in 1828 and in 1829 he was named Superintendent of the island of Fernando Po. Now called Bioka, the island off the west coast of Africa was a base for the Royal Navy's West Africa

Squadron as it tried to interdict the slave trade. Much as he had done in Florida, Major Nicolls used this posting to display great energy in the fight against slavery. He helped feed and organize liberated groups of slaves while also working to organize an alliance of West African countries to fight the slave trade. During his tour of duty in Florida, Nicolls had been accused by officials and citizens of the United States and Spain of enticing slaves to run away. He was accused of this activity by Portugal during his time on Fernando Po, but denied he had done so. He did write in 1842, however, that British law required him to liberate any slaves that made their way to the territory under his control. Although orders arrived for the major to return to England in 1832, it took three more years for him to complete his work on Fernando Po and sail for home.

Promoted to the rank of lieutenant colonel, Edward Nicolls retired from service in the Royal Marines on May 15, 1835. He was given a brevet promotion to the rank of colonel in 1840, postdated to 1837. In 1846 he was given brevet rank of major general and one year later was made a lieutenant general. Finally, in 1855, Nicolls became a full general. That same year he was honored with the title of Knight Commander of the Order of the Bath.

General Sir Edward Nicolls died at his home in London on February 5, 1865. He was 87 years old and was survived by his wife, Eleanor Bristow Nicolls, and four children, all daughters. Three other children, one daughter and two sons, had died earlier. One of these, Lieutenant Edward Nicolls served in the Royal Navy and gave his life aboard HMS *Dwarf* while trying to save the life of another man.

Historian Peter C. Smith, author of *Per Mare Per Terram: A History of the Royal Marines*, described General Nicolls as perhaps "the most distinguished officer the corps ever had." Future U.S. President John Quincy Adams, in a letter to President James Monroe, quoted Lord Bathurst as saying of then Colonel Nicolls that he was "a man of activity and spirit, but a very wild fellow."[1]

The following obituary appeared in the *Illustrated London News* on February 18, 1865:

This venerable officer, who died at his residence, 3, Woodland-terrace, Blackheath, on the 5th inst., was the son of Jonathan Nicolls, Esq., surveyor of Excise at Coleraine, Ireland, by his wife, Miss Cuppage, daughter of the Rev. Burke Cuppage, Rector of Coleraine. He was born at Coleraine, in 1779, and was educated at the grammar-school of that town and at the Royal Park Academy, Greenwich. He entered the Royal Marines at the age of sixteen, and was attached to the corps up to the period of his retirement. He became Colonel in 1837, and Lieutenant-General in 1854. In 1803 he distinguished himself by capturing a French armed cutter off St. Domingo with the aid of only thirteen volunteers, and on this occasion was severely wounded. He was at the passage of the Dardanelles, in 1807, and in several minor affairs, including the capture of an armed Italian gun-boat near Corfu, and at the reduction of Anholt, in the Cattegat. He was again severely wounded at the attack on Fort Bowyer, in 1814. He was created a K.C.B. in 1855. He married, in 1809, Mary, daughter of S. Bristow, Esq., and leaves issue.

Colonel Benjamin Hawkins

The resignation of Colonel Hawkins as U.S. Agent for Indian Affairs had been accepted by President James Monroe before he led his Creek army down the Chattahoochee River to confront the British at Nicolls' Outpost. Upon his return to the Georgia frontier, he continued to assist in concluding the business of the War of 1812. His reports to Governor Early describe conditions in the Creek Nation and mention final raids by the war parties sent out by the British.

Hawkins also engaged in a letter of wars with Colonel Nicolls during the final weeks of the British on the Apalachicola River. In these he accused the British officer of great cruelty to the people of the United States due to his actions in arming and supplying the Seminoles. The agent also correctly predicted that authorities in London would not ratify the treaty concluded at Nicolls' Outpost on March 10, 1815.

Benjamin Hawkins died at the Creek Agency on the Flint River near present-day Roberta on June 6, 1816. He was survived by his wife, Lavinia Downs, and seven children. His daughters bore the fascinating names Georgia, Muscogee, Cherokee, Carolina, Virginia and Jeffersonia. His son was named Madison. One of his nephews, Micajah Thomas Hawkins, because a U.S. Congressman from North Carolina.

Colonel Hawkins himself had served in the Continental Congress and U.S. Senate. During the American Revolution his knowledge of French attracted the attention of General George Washington who appointed Hawkins as his staff interpreter. The story of his life can be found today in the *Biographical Directory of the United States Congress:*

HAWKINS, Benjamin, (uncle of Micajah Thomas Hawkins), a Delegate and a Senator from North Carolina; born in what was then Granville, later Bute, and now Warren County, N.C., August 15, 1754; attended the county schools; student at the College of New Jersey (now Princeton University) when the Revolutionary War began; acquired a knowledge of French, and, at the request of General George Washington, left school and was appointed to the General's staff as his interpreter; member, State house of commons 1778-1779, 1784; chosen by the North Carolina legislature in 1780 to procure arms and munitions of war to defend the State; Member of the Continental Congress 1781-1783 and 1787; appointed by Congress to negotiate treaties with the Creek and Cherokee Indians in 1785; delegate to the State constitutional convention which ratified the Federal Constitution in November 1789; elected to the United States Senate and served from December 8, 1789, to March 3, 1795; appointed Indian agent for all the tribes south of the Ohio River by President Washington in 1796 and held the office until his death in Crawford County, Ga., on June 6, 1816; interment on a plantation near Roberta, Crawford County, overlooking the Flint River.[2]

Prophet Josiah Francis (Hillis Hadjo)

The Prophet returned to Florida from England by way of the Bahamas during the spring of 1817. His family by then was settled on the Wakulla River and he joined them there. Although authorities in London declined to recognize him as the ambassador of the Creek people, they did award him a colonelcy in the British army. While in Great Britain, Francis recognized the power of the written word and he arranged for his son Earle to remain behind so that he could receive a quality education.

Letters from Florida at the time of his return indicate that he urged the Seminoles and Red Sticks to be cautious and avoid provoking the Americans. When the First Seminole War erupted in November 1817, the Prophet led the American Indian army that assembled on the Apalachicola River. Warriors under his command waged the Battle of Ocheesee against a flotilla of U.S. supply vessels. Francis was not able to capture the boats, but his tactics led to major delays in the movement of the supplies intended for U.S. troops at Fort Scott, Georgia.

In late March 1818, as Major General Andrew Jackson's army was marching through Spanish Florida and destroying Creek and Seminole towns, Francis was at the Spanish fort of San Marcos de Apalache when ships appeared in Apalachee Bay flying the British flag. The prophet and a second Red Stick leader, Homathlemico, rowed out to the ships in a canoe, believing that desperately needed supplies had finally arrived from the British. The vessels, however, turned out to be American warships in disguise. The two leaders were taken prisoner and clapped in irons.

The great Creek Prophet Josiah Francis was hanged at the fort of San Marcos de Apalache on April 1, 1818. He pleaded that he be shot instead but the officers of Major General Andrew Jackson refused. Following his death, the executioners asked General Jackson what they should do with the prophet's body. The general responded that the Red Stick was no longer an enemy and to give him a proper burial. The location of the prophet's grave has been lost, but it is somewhere either on or near the grounds of San Marcos de Apalache Historic State Park in St. Marks, Florida.

Colonel Thomas Perryman

The old Seminole leader did not long survive the War of 1812. The son of an English trader named Theophilus Perryman and a Creek woman from the Eufaula town on the Chattahoochee River, he had lived his entire life on the lower Chattahoochee River and is one of the most misunderstood key figures of his time.

Confused by some writers for the Miccosukee leader Capachimico (Kenhajo), Perryman was a close ally of that important chief. One of his daughters married the pirate and adventurer William Augustus Bowles and it has been suggested that another was a wife of the British partisan Colonel Thomas Brown. The chief and his warriors fought as part of Brown's forces during the American Revolution and his military title of colonel dates from that era.

Thomas Perryman was an ally of William Augustus Bowles for many years and warriors from his village of Tocktoethla helped to fill the crews of Bowles' pirate ships. He later turned against the adventurer after Bowles threatened him.

A British soldier of the American Revolution and War of 1812, Thomas Perryman died in 1815-1816 and is buried in an unmarked grave somewhere in or near Fairchild Park in Seminole County, Georgia.

Brevet Major George Woodbine

Major Woodbine's career in the Colonial Marines came to an end as the War of 1812 drew to a close. He returned to the Bahamas as the British troops withdrew, but continued to lurk around Florida for the next two years. U.S.

officials accused Woodbine of having a plan to create an empire for himself among the American Indians. Whatever his intent, the trader turned officer turned trader was involved in several noted filibustering episodes. Woodbine was an ally of Sir Gregor McGregor who seized Fernandina and Amelia Island in 1817 only to lose them to the pirate/privateer Luis Aury a short time later.

Woodbine eventually settled into a life as a planter and merchant. By 1827 he was living on San Andres Island in the Caribbean. In that year a letter from him was forwarded to U.S. Secretary of State Henry Clay. It contained complaints against an American sea captain who was interfering with trade on the Indian Coast.

George Woodbine met a tragic fate on July 26, 1833:

On the night of the 26th July, Col. George W. Woodbine and his family, consisting of his wife and two sons, were inhumanly butchered at Maraparata, their plantation, about 2 leagues from Carthagena, near the shore of the Bay, in the direction of Boca Chica. The horrid act was supposed to be committed by blacks, from adjoining plantations, with the object of robbery. The dwelling was plundered of all the valuable furniture, and every part broken open and searched, where money would likely have been found – but it was believed none was found, as, after the murder, some gold, &c. belonging to the Colonel, was found deposited in another place. It was not known whether the Colonel's own slaves were accessory to the crime or not – they stated that they fled when the robbers attacked the premises, and the next day gave information of the act in Carthagena. Eighteen blacks residing in the neighborhood of the scene, have been arrested on suspicion, and were to have their trail the day after the Hesper sailed.[3]

One of the alleged assassins of Woodbine and his family testified against his co-conspirators. The killers included both men and women, all of whom had been the property of the former officer for many years and had been taken by him from Jamaica to San Andres and finally on to Carthagena.[4]

The murders sparked an international incident when local outrage boiled over after the French Consul made statements about Woodbine, his wife and child. Local authorities arrested the diplomat at the urging of prominent citizens:

...The Court of Justice declared that it was for the Superior Court to decide the matter, and this last mentioned court thought it prudent to order the Consul

to be set at liberty. Mr. Barrot, who was daily insulted in his own house, took the resolution of leaving the country and on his going to embark on a schooner lying in the port, he was in a most dastardly manner beaten and carried back to prison. I don't know how all this will end, and in what manner the French Government will take the treatment of its Consul, who they say is the brother of Odillon Barrot, a statesman of great influence in France....[5]

Tension resulting from the treatment of the French Consul reached its peak in November when two French warships appeared off Cartagena. After several days off the harbor, however, the two vessels sailed away.[6]

The assassins were executed on November 21, 1833. One woman, a slave named Leticia, was spared.[7]

Brigadier General William McIntosh (Tustunnuggee Hutkee)

McIntosh, the war chief of Coweta, had served as a major of U.S. Creek volunteers under Andrew Jackson during the Creek War of 1813-1814 and Colonel Hawkins during the Nicolls' Outpost expedition. The son of a white merchant and a Creek woman, he was the cousin of George Troup, who served as Governor of Georgia in 1823-1827.

A strong supporter of the "civilization plan" envisioned by the United States and Colonel Hawkins as a means of converting the Creeks from their traditional ways to white culture, McIntosh was called Tustunnuggee Hutkee "White Warrior" by his mother's people. He was a bitter enemy of Menawa and the Red Stick leaders that remained in the Nation after the Creek War.

Major McIntosh took part in the U.S. expedition against the Fort at Prospect Bluff in July 1816, leading hundreds of warriors from Coweta and other Lower Creek towns. He and his men surrounded the fort to block its land approaches while navy gunboats bombarded and destroyed it. The massive haul of British weapons and munitions found in the ruins added to the power of what became known as the McIntosh Faction of the Creeks.

His friendship with David Mitchell, who resigned the governor's chair in Georgia in 1817 to replace Hawkins as Agent for Indian Affairs, gave him great power over his political enemies. Mitchell was the father-in-law of one of the chief's daughters and the two men were close associates not only through the Creek Agency, but in their business and personal lives as well.

McIntosh entered the First Seminole War of 1817-1818 as the colonel of the U.S. Creek Brigade. He led more than 1,000 Creek soldiers down the

Chattahoochee River from Fort Mitchell in early 1818, snapping up Red Stick prisoners and destroying American Indian towns that had joined the alliance fighting against the United States. He defeated Econchattimico's warriors at the Battle of the Upper Chipola on March 13, 1818, before joining Andrew Jackson's main army in Middle Florida. He commanded Creek troops at the Battles of Econfina and Old Town. Jackson promoted him to the rank of brigadier general in recognition of his services.

William McIntosh signed away all remaining Creek lands in Georgia and his own life for $200,000 when he signed the second Treaty of Indian Springs on February 12, 1825. His cousin, George Troup, was then governor and had promised to protect the general and five other chiefs who signed the document against the wishes of their people. Creek law prohibited the sale of any lands to the whites without the approval of the entire nation.

The old Red Stick chief Menawa led around 200 warriors to carry out the execution of McIntosh and the five other leaders that had signed the treaty. The two were bitter enemies and for Menawa it was an opportunity for revenge. He had been disfigured by wounds at the Battle of Horseshoe Bend, escaping death only by swimming away underwater as bullets fell around him. William McIntosh had fought on the side of the United States in that battle.

Menawa's force found McIntosh at his Acorn Bluff (or Acorn Town) plantation on April 30, 1825. They shot and stabbed him to death, carrying out the execution ordered by the Creek Council. Another chief named Etomme Tustunnuggee was also executed and McIntosh's home was burned to the ground.

The McIntosh Inn, built by William McIntosh at Indian Springs in 1823, still stands today and can be seen in Butts County, Georgia. The McIntosh Reserve where he was killed is now a park in Carroll County, Georgia. His grave is marked by a boulder and a U.S. veterans' headstone.

Milly Francis

The youngest daughter of the Prophet Josiah Francis, Milly Francis was 12-years-old when the British abandoned Nicolls' Outpost and withdrew from the Apalachicola River. She moved with her mother and older sister to the Wakulla River for safety when her father and brother travelled to Great Britain with Colonel Nicolls.

Fluent in English and Spanish as well as the Alabama and Muscogee dialects, Milly became a friend of the daughters of the Spanish commandant at

San Marcos de Apalache. Eyewitness accounts describe her as an athletic young woman and one of the finest horseback riders in her village. When her father returned from England in 1817, he brought her numerous gifts including new London dresses and a saddle. By then she was 14-years-old and attracted the attention of Robert Ambrister, a former lieutenant from the Colonial Marines who was now associated with George Woodbine's filibustering efforts in Florida. Under the careful eye of her parents, the two developed a close friendship.

Milly was playing by the river with her sister when a captured Georgia militiaman named Duncan McCrimmon was brought to her village in the spring of 1818. Captured by two of the Prophet's warriors after he wandered away from Fort Gadsden, a new U.S. post built on the site of the earlier British fort at Prospect Bluff, McCrimmon was stripped naked and tied to a stake in the center of the village. Hearing the war cries of the warriors that captured the young soldier, Milly ran up into the village to investigate and realized that they were preparing to execute him.

Believing that McCrimmon was too young to have a "head for war," meaning that he was not old enough to make his own decisions, Milly asked her father to spare the young man's life. The Prophet responded, correctly, that he had no control over the soldier's fate. Creek Law placed McCrimmon's fate in the hands of the two warriors responsible for his capture, one of whom had lost his mother and the other a sister in the Creek War. Francis suggested that she speak to them.

Milly did so but found the two warriors resolute in their determination to kill Duncan McCrimmon. She reasoned with them by pointing out his young age and reminding them that killing the man would not bring back their lost loved ones. The two finally relented and agreed to spare the militiaman on the condition that he shave his head and agree to live as a Creek warrior.

Fearful that others in his town might not be so forgiving, Francis took McCrimmon to San Marcos de Apalache and turned him over to the Spanish commandant. The officer gave him freedom of the fort, but warned him not to stray beyond the walls as other warriors might kill him. Already under the protection of the Spanish soldiers were Edmund Doyle and William Hambly, the John Forbes & Company employees. They had been captured by Red Stick and Seminole forces at the Battle of Blunt's Town in 1817, but were spared through the intervention of the Black Seminole chief Nero, another former member of Nicolls' Colonial Marines.

McCrimmon and Milly were both present when her father was hanged by order of General Jackson. She also witnessed the execution of her friend Robert Ambrister by firing squad. When McCrimmon later offered to marry her in a show of gratitude for her having saved his life, she refused.

Milly returned to the Creek Nation in Alabama where she married a warrior and lived near Tallassee until the Trail of Tears in 1836. Her husband and other warriors volunteered to fight on behalf of the United States in the Second Seminole War and were away in Florida when U.S. troops arrived at Tallassee and ordered the Creek elderly, women and children to prepare to leave. They were marched on foot to Memphis, Tennessee. She later recalled that people along the route recognized her and were kind to her, giving food on which she and her children survived.

With the other survivors from their town, Milly and her children finally arrived at Fort Gibson in what is now Oklahoma. Marched out into the prairies in the bitter cold of January 1837, the Creeks were given one blanket per family and abandoned in the snow and ice. She built a crude cabin on a hill overlooking what is now Muskogee, Oklahoma, and lived out her life there. Her husband died from fever at Pass Christian, Mississippi, following his service against the Seminoles.

Milly died from tuberculosis after learning that she had been granted a pension and special medal of honor by the U.S. Congress in recognition of her heroism in saving the life of Duncan McCrimmon.[8]

Monuments have been erected in her honor on the grounds of Bacone College in Muskogee, a school for American Indians that now stands on the site of her home, and at San Marcos de Apalache Historic State Park in St. Marks, Florida. A historical marker tells her story at Fort Gadsden Historic Site in Florida's Apalachicola National Forest.*

Cappachimico

The old Miccosukee chief Cappachimico, also called Kenhadjo, continued to lead his large town on the western shore of Lake Miccosukee after the War of 1812. He tried to maintain peace with the United States and wished only to be left alone in Spanish Florida. U.S. troops, however, attacked the village of Fowltown in what is now Decatur County, Georgia, on November 21 and 23,

* For her complete story, please read *Milly Francis: The Life & Times of the Creek Pocahontas* by this author.

1817. Fowltown was closely allied with Miccosukee and the deaths of several warriors and a woman in the attacks ignited outrage among Cappachimico's warriors. They subsequently took part in the First Seminole War, joining in the attacks along the Apalachicola River in late 1817.

The role of the Miccosukees in the slaying of 34 soldiers, 6 women and 4 children led by Lieutenant Richard W. Scott of the 7th U.S. Infantry made their town a key target of Major General Andrew Jackson's 1818 invasion of Florida. U.S. forces attacked Miccosukee on April 1, 1818, but a delaying action by some of the warriors gave Cappachimico time to evacuate most of his people across Lake Miccosukee to safety. Over 200 homes were destroyed and hundreds of head of cattle were confiscated by Jackson's troops.

Cappachimico was reported killed in the battle, but this was obviously due to mistaken identity as he was alive and with his people when the First Seminole War came to an end a few months later. He died of natural causes prior to the cession of Florida from Spain to the United States in 1821.

Captain William Perryman

A veteran of the British service in both the American Revolution and War of 1812, Captain William Perryman was the son of Colonel Thomas Perryman and the brother-in-law of the pirate and adventurer William Augustus Bowles. He returned to his village of Tellmochesses on the west side of the Chattahoochee River in what is now Jackson County, Florida, after the British withdrew from the Apalachicola.

Realizing that the British would never return, Perryman worked to forge better relations with the United States. After the death of his father he ascended to the leadership of both of the Perryman towns and Tocktoethla was moved across the river into Spanish Florida at a new site south of Tellmochesses, which stood about 15 miles north of today's Sneads, Florida. When the First Seminole War erupted in 1817, the Perryman warriors sided with the United States against many of the other towns of the old British alliance.

Learning that the Red Sticks were planning to attack Blunt's Town, the village of Chief John Blunt, William Perryman led his men down the river to protect the chief and the traders Edmund Doyle and William Hambly. He was killed in the Battle of Blunt's Town on December 10, 1817. Members of the Perryman family, however, later ascended to the leadership of the Creek or Muscogee Nation in Oklahoma.

[1] Peter C. Smith, *Per Mare Per Terram: A History of the Royal Marines*, St Ives Press, 1974; Secretary of State John Quincy Adams to President James Monroe, September 19 1815, British and Foreign State Papers, 1818-1819, James Ridgway, London, 1835, p. 368.

[2] "Hawkins, Benjamin (1754-1816)", *Biographical Directory of the United States Congress*, http://bioguide.congress.gov.

[3] Description of the death of George Woodbine by Capt. Beekman of the merchant ship *Hesper*, published in the *Alexandria Gazette*, September 5, 1833, p. 2.

[4] *Connecticut Gazette*, September 11, 1833, p. 3.

[5] Letter from Cartagena, August 25, 1833, published in the *Charleston Courier*, October 17, 1833, p.2.

[6] *Ibid.*

[7] *Ibid.*

[8] Dale Cox, *Milly Francis: The Life & Times of the Creek Pocahontas*, Old Kitchen Books, 2014.

Abraham, a member of Nicolls' Colonial Marines

Capt. Timpoochee Barnard, Hawkins' Yuchi Company

Neamathla, Chief of Fowltown and a member of Nicolls' force

Major William McIntosh, Hawkins' Creek Brigade

Gov. Peter Early of Georgia

Sam and Ben Perryman, Creek Warriors
Courtesy of the Library of Congress

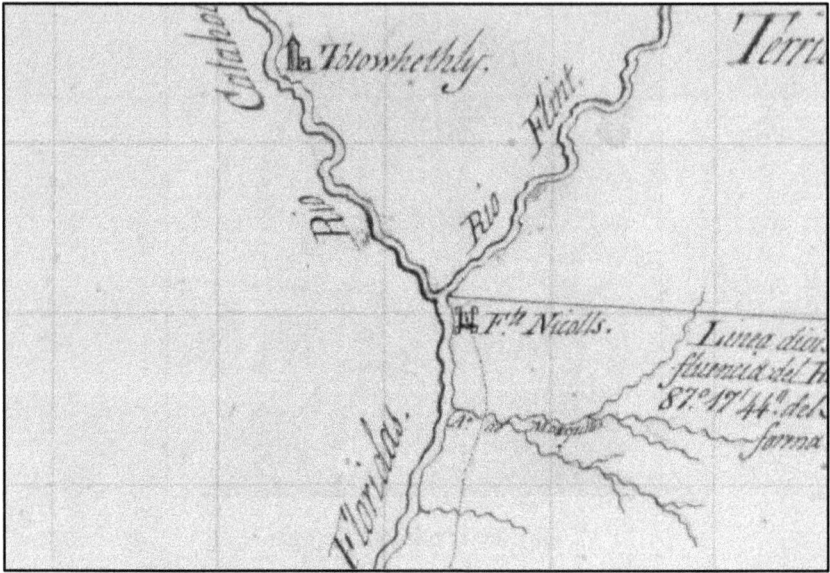

Nicolls' Outpost, from Pintado Map of 1815
West Florida History Center, University of West Florida

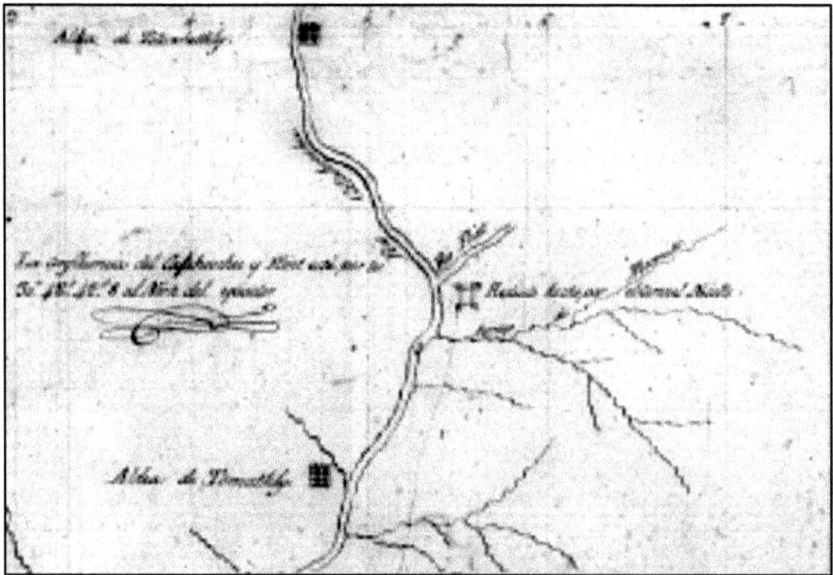

Nicolls' Outpost, from Pintado Map of 1817
West Florida History Center, University of West Florida

Confluence of the Chattahoochee and Flint Rivers as it appears today

Apalachicola River from the site of Nicolls' Outpost

Christopher Kimball (L) and Lionel Young portray the Prophet Francis and Col. Benjamin Hawkins at the dedication of the Nicolls' Outpost marker.

Nicolls' Outpost marker unveiling in Chattahoochee, Florida.

Nicolls' Outpost: A War of 1812 Fort at Chattahoochee, Florida

Apalachicola River and landing site at Nicolls' Outpost

Aerial view of Nicolls' Outpost site in Chattahoochee, Florida

Osceola was among the young children sheltered by the British at the forts on the Apalachicola. He and his mother were part of Peter McQueen's band and he grew to become the best known Seminole warrior of the 19th century.
George Catlin sketch courtesy of the Library of Congress.

APPENDICES

APPENDIX ONE

PROCLAMATION by Lieutenant-Colonel Edward Nicolls, commanding his Brittanic Majesty's forces in the Floridas.

Natives of Louisiana! – On you the first call is made to assist in liberating from a faithless and imbecile government your paternal soil.

Spaniards, Frenchmen, Italians, and British, whether settled, or residing for a time in Louisiana, on you also I call to aid me in this just cause. The American usurpation in this country must be abolished, and the lawful owners of this soil put in possession. I am at the head of a large army of Indians, well armed, disciplined, and commanded by British officers, a good train of artillery, with every requisite, seconded by a powerful aid of a numerous British and Spanish squadron of ships and vessels of war. Be not alarmed, inhabitants of the country, at our approach: the same good faith and disinterestedness which has distinguished the conduct of Britons in Europe accompanies them here : you will have no fear of litigious taxes imposed on you for the purpose of carrying on unnatural and unjust war; your property, your laws, the peace and tranquility of your country, will be guaranteed to you by men who will suffer no infringement of their's. Rest assured that these brave men only burn with an ardent desire of satisfaction, for the wrongs they have suffered from the Americans, to join you in liberating these southern frontiers from their yoke, and drive them into those limits formerly prescribed by my Sovereign. The Indians have pledged themselves, in the most solemn manner, not to injure, in the slightest degree, persons or properties of any but enemies to their Spanish or English Fathers. A flag over any door, whether Spanish, French, or British, will be a certain protection. Not even an enemy will an Indian put to death, except resisting his arms; and as for injuring helpless women, and children, and old men, by their good conduct and treatment to them, they will, if it be possible, make the Americans blush for their more than inhuman conduct, lately on the Escambia and within a neutral territory. Inhabitants of Kentucky, you have too long borne with grievous impositions; the whole brunt of the war has fallen on your brave sons: be imposed on no more, but either range yourselves under the standard of your forefathers, or observe a strict neutrality. If you comply with either of these offers, whatever provisions you send down, will be paid for in dollars, and the safety of the persons bringing it, as well as the free navigation of the Mississippi guaranteed to you. Men of Kentucky, let me call to your view, and I trust to your abhorrence, the conduct of those factions which hurried you into this cruel, unjust, and unnatural war, at a time when Great Britain was straining every nerve in defence of her own, and the liberties of the world; - when the bravest of her sons were fighting and bleeding in so sacred a cause; when she was spending millions of her treasure in endeavoring to pull down one of the most formidable and dangerous tyrants that ever disgraced the form of man: - when groaning Europe was almost at her last gasp – when she alone shewed an undaunted front, basely did those assassins endeavour to stab her from her race. She has turned on them, renovated from the bloody but successful struggle. Europe is happy and free, and she now hastens justly to avenge the unprovoked insults. Shew them that you are not collectively unjust: leave that contemptible few to shift for themselves; let these slaves of the Tyrant send an embassy to Elba, and implore his aid, but let every honest upright American spurn them with merited contempt. After the experience of 21 years, can you any longer support these brawlers for licentiousness, who call it freedom? Be no longer their dupes; accept my offer; every thing I have promised in this paper, I guarantee you on the sacred honour of a British Officer.

Given under my hand, at my Head-quarters, Pensacola, this 29th of August, 1814.

EDWARD NICOLLS.

APPENDIX TWO

The Prophet Josiah Francis & Peter McQueen to Hon. Sir Alexander Cochrane, K.B.

Great and illustrious Warrior,

We have received the letter you sent to us by Colonel Nicolls. You say well, great Chief, that our breasts are filled with the glorious love of liberty, and, protected by our great and good father, we will live or die free, of which we have given hard proof, by choosing to abandon our country rather than live in it as slaves. We thank you for the supplies you have sent and promised to send; we receive them with unbounded gratitude : but for them we should all have perished. Be pleased to send our love and duty to our good and great father, King George. He has shown that he has not forgot his once happy children, and we bless the Great Spirit for freeing him from his enemies in Europe. Our long absence from him we liken to the longings of a father for a lost son; our happiness, like a father who has found one. Your sons whom you have sent to our aid we hail as brothers on the shores of the sea, but we hope soon to embrace them in the land of our forefathers. Our distress has been beyond the power of our tongues to tell you; we were driven from our homes, and our clothes and household utensils taken from us. From that time until we took your sons by the hand, famine, nakedness, and their accompanying miseries have been our lot. Our fathers were true men to your fathers; they told us to be so always. They are dead, but their truth remains with us, and we implore our good father to continue his paternal assistance, for we have fought and bled in his cause. Pray of him, great chief, to keep a port on this coast, for the Spaniards are weak, frail friends. In our time of distress they turned us into the woods like dogs, but since your sons came here we walk like men in their streets. The chief you have sent to us we receive as we ought; we will obey him in all things. We have made him our kind warrior and Commander in Chief. We will get all the black men we can to join your warriors. We thank you also for your promise of protecting our rights on a general peace taking place. We will do our best to unite all our red brethren, and form a strong arm, that will be ready to crush the wicked and rebellious Americans when they shale dare to insult our father and his children. We hope you will always keep a chief here with us, for as long as he stays among us, our ways will be shown to us, and we will walk in them. We pray to the Great Spirit for, and give our blessings to your father, and to you, and tell him we will fight bravely under his colours.

In the name of our broughters,
their

JOHN X FRANCIS, Warrior of Tuskeege.
PETER X MC QUIN, Warrior of Talase.
marks.

To the Hon. Sir. Alexander Cochrane, K.B.
Vice-Admiral of the Red, &c. &c. &c.

Appendix Three

Letter from Sir Alexander Cochrane, to the Great and Illustrious Chiefs of the Creek and Other Indian Nations.

Hear! O ye brave Chiefs of the Creek and other Indian Nations.

The great King George, our beloved father, has long wished to assuage the sorrows of his warlike Indian children, and to assist them in gaining their rights and possessions from their base and perfidious oppressors.

The trouble our father has had in conquering his enemies beyond the great waters, he has brought to a glorious conclusion; and peace is again restored amongst all the nations of Europe.

The desire, therefore, which he has long felt, of assisting you, and the assurance which he has given you of his powerful protection, he has now chosen as is chiefs by sea and land to carry into effectual execution.

Know then, O Chiefs and Warriors, that in obedience to the Great Spirit which directs the soul of our Mighty Father, we come with a power which it were vain for all the people of the United States to oppose. Behold the great waters covered with our ships, from which will go forth an army of warriors, as numerous as the whole Indian nations; inured to the toils and hardships of war – accustomed to triumph over all opposition – the constant favourites of victory.

The same principle of justice which le dour father to wage a war of 20 years in favour of the oppressed nations of Europe, animates him now in support of his Indian children; and by the efforts of his warriors, he hopes to obtain for them the restoration of those lands of which the people of the bad spirit have lately robbed them.

We promised you by our talk of last June, that great fleets and armies were coming to attack our foes : and you will have heard of our having triumphantly taken their capital city of Washington, as well as many other places – beaten their armies in battle, and spread terror over the heart of their country.

Come forth then, ye brave chiefs and warriors, as one family, and join the British standard – the signal of union between the powerful and oppressed – the symbol of justice, led on by victory.

If you want covering to protect yourselves, your wives and your children, against the winter's cold, - come to us, and we will cloth you. If you want arms and ammunition to defend yourselves against your oppressors, - come to us, and we will provide you. Call around you the whole of your Indian brethren – and we will show them the same tokens of our brotherly love.

And what think you we ask in return for this bounty of our Great Father, which we his chosen warriors have so much pleasure in offering to you? Nothing more than that you should assist us manfully in regaining your lost lands – the lands of your forefathers – from the common enemy, the people of the United States; and that you should hand down these lands to your children hereafter, as we hope we shall now be able to deliver them up to you, we have forced our enemies to ask for a peace, our good Father will on no account forget the welfare of his much-lov'd Indian children.

Again then, brave Chiefs, and warriors of the Indian nation, at the mandate of the Great Spirit, we call upon you to come forth arrayed in battle to fight the great fight of justice, and recover your long-lost freedom. Animate your hearts in this sacred cause – unite with us as the sons of one common father, - and a great and glorious victory will shortly crown our exertions.

Given under our hands and seals on board his Brittanic Majesty's ship Tonnant, off Appalachicolo.

ALEX. COCHRANE.
JOHN KEANE.
Dec. 5, 1814.

Appendix Four

Treaty of Nicolls' Outpost

ADDRESS OF THE INDIANS TO THE KING OF ENGLAND, ON THE CONCLUSION OF THE TREATY OF PEACE.

We, the Chiefs of the Muscogee nation, in full council assembled, on behalf of ourselves and our people, do make the following requests of our good father King George, and declare to him certain resolutions we have come to, with our reasons for so doing.

We conceive it to be indispensably necessary for our good, as well as to make us useful allies of Great Britain, that British officers should be kept constantly among us, and we request that our good father will grant us this favour. Since Colonel Brown left us, we have been a prey to civil dissensions, fomented and kept up by our inveterate and never-to-be-satisfied foe, the Americans by their bad advice has brother been in the act of shedding the blood of brother: and when the land becomes thus desolated, they possess themselves of it, so that we shall soon be driven to the desert sands of the sea, from the fertile of our forefathers; and we are told that the Spaniards will not let us trade with the British from the mouths of our rivers: we, therefore, further request, that our good father will secure for us the mouths of the rivers Apilachicola, Alibama, and St. Mary's; for, if our communication is once more cut off from his children, we shall be totally ruined; we have fought and bled for him against the Americans, by which we have made them our more bitter enemies, and as he has stood the friend of the oppressed nations beyond the great waters, he will surely not forget the sufferings of his once happy children here. We therefore rely on his future protection and his fatherly kindness: we will truly keep the talks which his chief has given us, if he is graciously pleased to continue his protection: famine is now devouring up ourselves and our children, by reason of our Upper Town brethren being driven down upon us in the time the corn was green, and now their miseries and necessities cause them to root up the seed of our future crop, so that we sow in the day we are obliged to watch at night.

Was it not for the powder we get from your chief, the whole of the nation would be in dust: the Red Sticks have shot and eat up almost the whole of our cattle, for they have seen their children digging in the woods for want, and who can blame them, when they are pressed by such cruel necessity? Thus are we situated, and are only looking to the departure or the stay of your children, as the signal of our destruction or prosperity. In former times, after the British left us, to show our love and regard for their nation, we made a grant of their lands to the house of Panton, Leslie, and Co., and latterly, to the house of John Forbes and Co., on certain terms; that they were to settle the lands with British men, and to keep up a sufficient and good assortment of all sorts of merchandise suitable to our wants; but instead of their doing this, they have attempted to settle our lands with Americans, and have refused to supply us with powder, when we were attacked by our enemies, and have urged us to declare for the Americans against the British,, and have offered rewards to us for that purpose; and they have actually written to their agents who reside among us, desiring them to obstruct the British officers all in their power from assisting us, and to represent to them, alas, how impossible it would be for them to succeed against the Americans, and we having intercepted their letters, did deliver them to Lieut. Colonel Nicholls, who is our witness; and the said letters were delivered to an Indian by John Forbes, at St. Augustine, to be forwarded by him as aforesaid; and as it does stand thus, on unquestionable proof, that the said house of Forbes and Co. have shamefully broken their contracts with us, we do, in this our full assembly, declare all their property in our nation to be confiscated to the nation : and we further annul and declare void our grant or grants of land accordingly, warning them and all belonging to them never to appear again in the nation. And the United States of America, or some part thereof, have thought proper to run a line or waggon road through the Indian nation, from Hartford in Georgia, to Mobile in West Florida, without our consent, and to our great hurt and annoyance. We do implore our good Father that he will cause them to disuse the said road, and to cease all communication between them and us, as we are determined to cease having any communication with them; and we warn all Americans to keep out of this nation. And whereas a young chief called McIntosh was sent with a message of remonstrance against the above-mentioned road being run, and of several other enchroachments being made on the Tombigby, Cooza, and Alibama rivers, instead of his making such remonstrance, he suffered himself to be tricked by our enemy, and unlawfully sold to them a large tract of land on and about the rivers Aconee, Oakemulgee, which tracts of land we implore our good Father to use his endeavour in getting restoration of them, The above-mentioned McIntosh holds a commission as Major in the American army, and of the Creek Regiment: he has caused much blood to be spilt, for which we denounce him to the whole nation, and will give the usual reward of the brave who may kill him, he having on a recent occasion killed and scalped a brother who was on an errand of peace to our Cherokee brethren, for now other reason alleged against him than his having British arms about him, and in this we are told he has been encouraged by Colonel Hawkins, although long after a peace was declared, and all hostility ordered to cease.

We further request Lieut.-Col. Nicolls will return our grateful thanks to our good Father and his chiefs by sea and land, for the useful and good presents he has sent to us by them; and also that the Lieut.-Colonel, and the officers with him in this nation, will receive our thanks for their brotherly conduct to us: and whereas our good Father having made a peace with the United States of America, and according to his true talk, he has not forgotten the interests of us, his children, but has caused to be respected our lands, and guaranteed the integrity of them to us; we do declare them or him to be traitors to this nation who shall, without his or our consent, sell or make over to any foreign power, any part thereof : and we do further declare, that whosoever shall endeavour directly or indirectly to separate us from him, or his children, to be the enemy of us and our children, and that we will not trade or barter with any other than the British nation, if the above requests be complied with ; and we do promise to give grants of land to all such British men as our good Father shall give permission to stay among us, and that we will do our best to protect and defend them in their laws and property : and we send as our representative, our brave brother Hidlis Hadgo (Francis) to our good Father, who is authorized to ratify this treaty.

Given under our hands at the British Fort, at the confluence of the Chatutouchee and Flint rivers, this 10th March, 1815.

HOPOATH MICO, King of the 4 nations, X mark.
HOPOY MICO, X T.P.   ACOPCHIGE MATHO X
NEHEMATHLA X   TATAO MICO X
JUSTOMIC HAGO X   HOPOATHLA TUSTANUGGEE X
ONUS HAGO X

NEHEMATHLA, 2d X   CONOPE MATHLA X
NEHEMATHLA, 3d X   YATOULE MATHLA X
JUSTOMIC EMATHLA X   JOHNSON X
OCTAITHGE HAGO X HIDLIS HADGO X
And 14 other Chiefs.

[Witness]   ED. NICOLLS, Lieutenant-Colonel.
            H.ROSS, Captain Rifle Corps.
            JOS. ROCHE, Captain 1st West India Reg.
            WM. HAMBLY, Lieut. And 1st Interpreter.

APPENDIX FIVE

Correspondence between Col. Nicolls & Col. Hawkins

March 19, 1815
Col. Benjamin Hawkins to Lt. Col. Edward Nicolls
Washington (KY) *Union*, June 30, 1815, p. 2.

Creek Agency, 19th March, 1815.

I have received yours of the 7th, and cannot subscribe to your construction of the voluntary invitation sent by captain Henry to the people of the Creek nation, whose slaves were with you. Your restriction leaves nothing for it to operate on, and he could not have so intended it. You will see in the first article of the treaty of peace that provision is made against carrying away slaves and other private property, such as that in question.

Being the medium of communication between your superior officers and you on the restoration of peace, as well as the officer of the United States in this quarter charged with their Indian affairs, I must and do protest against your carrying away any negroes belonging to Indians within the United States or citizens thereof, and require that they be so left on your embarkation as that their proper owners may get possession of them.

April 28, 1815
Lt. Col. Edward Nicolls to Benjamin Hawkins
Western Citizen, July 8, 1815, p. 1.

Appalachicola,, 28th April.

Being absent from this post when your letter of the 19th ult. arrived, I take this opportunity to answer it. On the subject of the negroes lately owned by citizens of the United States or Indians in hostility to the British forces, I have to acquaint you, that according to orders, I have sent them to the British colonies, where they are received as free settlers, and lands given to them. The newspaper you sent me is, I rather think, incorrect; at all events an American newspaper cannot be authority for a British officer. I herewith enclose you a copy of a part of the 9th article of the treaty of peace relative to the Indians in alliance with us, they have signed and accepted it as an independent people, solemnly protesting to suspend all hostilities against the inhabitants of the United States. Within these few days I have had a complaint from the Seminole chief, Bow Legs. He states that a party of American horse had made an incursion into his town, killed one man, wounded another, and stole some of his cattle – also, that they have plundered some of his people on their peaceable way from St. Augustine. May I request of you to inquire into this affair, and cause justice to be done to the murderer. I strickly promise you that for any mischief done by the Creeks under me, I shall do all in my power to punish the delinquents and have the property restored.

The chiefs here have requested me further to declare to you (that in order to prevent any disagreeable circumstance from happening in the future) they have come to a determination not to permit the least intercourse between their people and those of the United States. They have in consequence ordered them to cease all communication directly or indirectly with the territory or citizens of the United States – and they do take this public mode of warning the citizens of the United States, from entering their territory or communicating directly or indirectly with the Creek people. They also request that you will understand their territories to be as they stood in the year 1811. In my absence I have directed first lieutenant Wm. Hambly, the head interpreter, to communicate with you on any point relative to the Creeks: and I have given him my most positive orders, that he shall at all times do his best to keep peace and good neighborhood between the Creeks and your citizens.

I am sir, your very humble servant,
EDWARD NICOLLS.
Commanding the British Forces in the Floridas.

Enclosure:

We the undersigned, chiefs of the Muscogee nation, declared by his Britannic majesty to be a free and independent people, do in the name of the said nation agree to the 9th article of the treaty of peace between his Britannic majesty and the United States – and we do further declare that we have given the most strict and positive orders to all our people that they desist from hostilities of every king against the citizens or subjects of the United States.

Given under our hands at the British fort on the Appalachicola, the 2d day of April, 1815.

HEPOOETH MICCO`   X.
CAPPACHIMICO   X.
HOPOY MECCO   T.P.

May 12, 1815
Lt. Col. Edward Nicolls to Col. Benjamin Hawkins[*]
Georgia Journal, June 7, 1815, p. 3.

British Post, Appalachicola river,
May 12th, 1815.

In my letter to you on the 28th ult. I requested you would be so good as to make enquiry into the murder and robberies committed on the Seminoles belonging to the Chief called Bow-Legs, at the same time declaring to you my determination of punishing with utmost rigor of the law any one of our side who broke it. Of this a melancholy proof has been given in the execution of an Indian of the Atophalga town by Hothly Poya Tustunnuggee, Chief of the Ocmulgees, who found him driving off a gang of cattle belonging to your citizens, and for which act of justice I have given him double presents and a Chief's gun, in the open square before the whole of the Chiefs, and highly extolled him. These, sir, are the steps I am daily taking to keep the peace with sincerity; but I am sorry to say that the same line is not taken on your side, nor have you written to me to say what steps you are taking or intend to take to secure this mutual good. Since the last complaint from Bow-Legs I have had another from him to say your citizens have again attacked and murdered two of his people – that they had stolen a gang of his cattle, but that he had succeeded in regaining them. I asked them what proof they had of the people being killed. They said they had

---

[*] Note: Written two days before the British evacuated the Apalachicola River.

found their bloody clothes in the American camp, which was hastily evacuated on their approach. Now sir, if these enormities are suffered to be carried on in a Christian country, what are you to expect by shewing such an example to the uncultivated native of the woods – (for savage I won't call them, their conduct entitles them to a better epithet.) I have, however, ordered them to stand on the defensive, and have sent them a large supply of arms and ammunition, and told them to put to death without mercy any one molesting them; but at all times to be careful not to put a foot over the American line. In the mean time that I should complain to you – that I was convinced you would do your best to curb such infamous conduct. – Also, that those people who did such deeds would (I was convinced) be disowned by the government of the United States, and severely punished. They have given their consent to await your answer before they take revenge; but sir, they are impatient for it, & well armed as the whole nation now is, and stored with ammunition and provisions, having a strong hold to retire upon in case of a superior force appearing. Picture to yourself sir, the miseries that may be suffered by good and innocent citizens on your frontiers, and I am sure you will lend me your best aid in keeping the bad spirits in subjection. Yesterday in a full assembly of the Chiefs, I got them to pass a law for four resolute Chiefs to be appointed in different parts of the nation something in the character of our Sheriffs, for the purpose of inflicting condign punishment on such people as broke the law, and I will say this much for them, that I never saw men execute laws better than they do. I am also desired to say to you by the chiefs, that they do not find your citizens are evacuating their lands according to the 9th article of the treaty of peace; but that they were fresh provisioning the Forts. This point, sir, I beg of you to look into. They also request me to inform you, that they have signed a treaty of offensive and defensive alliance with Great Britain, as well as one of commerce and navigation, which as soon as it is ratified at home you shall be made more fully aquainted with.

May 28, 1815
Col. Benjamin Hawkins to Lt. Col. Edward Nicolls[*]
Augusta Herald, June 15, 1815, p. 2.

---

[*] The British had left the Apalachicola by the date of this letter. Col. Nicolls never saw it.

Creek Agency, 28th May, 1815.

On the 24th I wrote to you in reply to your's of the 28th ult. and since have had the pleasure to receive yours of the 12th. I had received from Bow-Legs direct, a complaint of an outrage committed "by the people of Georgia who had gone into East-Florida, driven off his cattle and destroyed his property." I have sent this complaint to the Governor of Georgia, who will readily co-operate with the officers of the General Government, to cause justice to be done the injured, if the complaint is true. The laws of the United States provide completely for the protection of the Indian rights, and those interested with their execution have the power of doing it. All that is wanted is proof against the transgressors.

The Indians of Aulotchewau, who without provocation murdered and plundered a number of subjects of Spain on St. Johns, have engendered such a deadly feud between the parties, that it will be long before the descendants of the injured can forget and forgive. Spain, from her in-interval commotions, has not found it convenient to settle a peace between them, and these people it is probable are mistaken for Georgians. The Indians of this Agency, as well as those in Florida, have long known they are to apply through their Chiefs to me for a redress of their grievances. The government of the Creeks is not an ephemeral one. Its last modification is of more than ten years standing. It was the work and choice of the nation, and has a check on the conduct of the Seminoles.

In 1799 a gentleman [*i.e.* William Augustus Bowles] arrived where you are from England, who had been an officer on half pay. He came in the Fox sloop of war, furnished by the Admiral on the Jamaica station by order of the Admiralty, "to facilitate him a passage to his nation the Creeks." This gentlemen after attempting in various ways with the Seminoles, to usurp the government of the Creeks without success, created himself Director General of Muscogee, declared war against Spain, murdered some of her subjects and took St. Marks. He ordered me with my assistants in the plan of civilization out of the Creek Nation.

I communicated his proceedings to the national councils who had been previously acquainted with him, and who replied to him, "that he had a title among them which he well merited Cap,pe,tun,nee,lox,au (the Prince of Liars) and no other." The Director General of Muscogee, after playing a farce for two years, experienced a tragic scene, which deprived him of his liberty. He was put in irons by order of the Council whose government he tried to usurp, and sent to the Governor General of Louisiana to answer for his crimes. His Seminoles Chiefs were glad to retire with impunity. After this it was unanimously determined by the National Council of distinguished Chiefs from every town, and a deputation of Choctaws, Chickasaws and Cherokees, that the warriors should be glassed and held in readiness to execute the orders of the Executive council; and that the Agent for Indian Affairs should have the power of executing the treaty stipulations of the Creeks with their white neighbors. Tookaubatche and Cowetau alternately as the occasion required was appointed the permanent seat of their national councils, where national affairs alone could be transacts. They have now two speakers – When the Council meets at Cowetau, Tustunnugee Hopoi [*i.e.* Little Prince], as Speaker for the Lower Creeks, is Speaker for the Nation, and when they meet at Tookaubatche, Tustunnugge Thlucco [*i.e.* Big Warrior] of the upper Creeks is speaker for the Nation – Cowetau is head quarters for the present. The agent for Indian Affairs can convene the Council.

To this council I communicated in your own words the pretensions of your three chiefs. They answer – "We have had Col. Nicolls' communication before us – that Hopoith Micco, Caupuchau Micco and Hopoie Micco are the soverigns of this nation. We know nothing about them as such. We have often invited them to attend our talks. They never would come forward, and Hopohieth Micco is a hostile Indian. They have nothing to do with our affairs. They reside in the Spanish territory."

After mentioning a solitary effort of yours to "keep the peace," you say "I am sorry to say the same line is not taken on your side, nor have you written to me to say what steps you are taking or intend to take to secure this mutual good." You should not have expected I should communicate with you, when from your orders you were so soon to leave the country. I have communicated to the national council several outrages committed by banditties from the Seminoles, and other parts, upon the post road and frontiers of Georgia, repeatedly. They have in two instances had the guilty shot, and sent armed parties after others. As late as the 17th April one man was killed and four wounded on the post road. Our waggons twice attacked and one waggoner killed, several horses taken and carried as reported, to your depot at the very time the waggons were carrying seed corn for the Indians and flour for the support of nearly 5000 entirely destitute of food.

The measures in operations here to preserve peace is with an efficient force, red and white troops, to pursue, apprehend and punish all violators of the public peace. The Executive Council of the Creeks are continually at Cowetau with an Assistant Agent to take orders with the warriors when the necessity is apparent, and to call on me when the aid of regular troops is necessary. We do not rely on the exertions of any one but ourselves, to preserve peace among the Creeks, and between them and their neighbors of the United States and the Floridas. We examine fairly, spare the innocent and punish the guilty; and in no case to suffer revenge to carve for itself.

On an exparte hearing, you have "armed the Seminoles and given orders to put to death without mercy every one molesting them." This is cruelty without example, scalping men, women and children, for trouble or vexing only, and the executioners the judges. To gratify their revenge, the good & innocent citizens on the frontiers are to be the victims of such barbarity. Suppose a banditti of white people were to commit a violent outrage, such as that of the 17th April, are we to charge it on the unoffending people on the frontiers, and kill them without mercy, if we could not find the guilty? You have issued the order, provided & issued munitions of war for its execution, prepared and provisioned a stronghold to retire upon, in case of a superior force appearing, to protect them in this mode of gratifying their revenge. You will be held responsible and your strong holds will certainly not avail. If you are really on the service of his Britannic Majesty, it is an act of hostility which will require to be speedily met and speedily crushed. But sir, I am satisfied that you are acting from yourself on some speculative project of your own. The Sovereign of Great Britain could not from his love of justice in time of peace, his systematic perseverance in support of legitimate Sovereigns, almost to the impoverishing of his own nation, suffer any of his officers to go into a neutral country to disturb its peace.

If the Seminolie Indians have complaints to make, they will do it through the Chiefs of the Creek Nation, or direct to me or through an officer of his Catholic Majesty as heretofore, I will cause justice to be done. In cases of murder, the guilty if practicable, shall be punished, in cases of theft restitution shall be made.

The treaties you have made for the Creek Nation, with the authority created by yourself for the purpose, must be a novelty. It would surprise me much to see your Sovereign ratify such as you have described them to be, with a people such as I know those to be, in the territories of his Catholic Majesty – I shall communicate what has passed on the subject between us to the officers of Spain in my neighborhood, that they may be apprised of what you are doing.

As you may not have recent news from Europe, I send you some news-papers detailing important events there to the 4th April.

I am, &c.

BENJAMIN HAWKINS,
Agent for Indian Affairs.

REFERENCES

Letters & Reports

British

Anonymous to Lt. Jackson, HMS Cockchafer, July 19, 1814, Cochrane Papers.

Anonymous, extract of a letter from a gentleman at Pensacola to his correspondent in New Orleans, July 25, 1814, *Louisiana Gazette*, August 16, 1814.

Anonymous, Report from Halifax, Nova Scotia, dated March 29, 1815, published by the Lexington, Kentucky, *Reporter*, May 10, 1815, p. 3.

Earl Bathurst to Gov. Charles Cameron, January 21, 1814, Public Records Office, Colonial Office, 24/14.

Gov. Charles Cameron to Earl Bathurst, October 28, 1813, Public Records Office, Colonial Office, 23/60.

Cappachimico and other chiefs, Address of the Indians to the King of England, on the Conclusion of the Treaty of Peace, March 10, 1815, *London Times*, August 13, 1818.

Rear Admiral George Cockburn to the Chief of any Indian tribe on or near the Border of Georgia, March 10, 1815, Hargrett Rare Book and Manuscript Library, The University of Georgia Libraries, Telamon Cuyler Collection, Box 82, Folder 18, Document 01 (signed aboard the HMS Albion off Cumberland Island).

Edward Codrington, letter dated December 14, 1814, in *Memoir of the Life of Admiral Sir Edward Codrington* (Abridged edition), p. 239.

Joshua [sic.] Francis and others to British Commander at St. George's Island, June 9, 1814, Cochrane Papers.

Lt. Edward Handfeld to Gov. Charles Cameron, October 28, 1813, Public Records Office, Colonial Office, 23/60.

Capt. Robert Henry to Admiral Alexander Cochrane, November 22, 1814, Cochrane Papers.

Bvt. Major Edward Nicolls to Admiral Alexander Cochrane, August 12, 1814, Cochrane Papers.

Lt. Col. Edward Nicolls to Admiral Alexander Cochrane, August-November 1814, Cochrane Papers.

Lt. Col. Edward Nicolls to Capt. Robert Henry, December 4, 1814, original document in Carswell Collection.

Lt. Col. Edward Nicolls to Rear Admiral Percy Malcolm, February-March 1815, Cochrane Papers.

Lt. Col. Edward Nicolls, December 19, 1815, Public Record Office, London, England, Colonial Office.

Col. Thomas Perryman, Capt. William Perryman, Alexander Durant and Noah Hoeo to Governor of Providence, September 11, 1813, Public Records Office, Colonial Office, 23/60.

Capt. Hugh Pigot to Capt. George Woodbine, May 5, 1814, Cochrane Papers (Signed aboard HMS Orpheus)

Capt. Hugh Pigot to Capt. George Woodbine, May 10, 1814, Cochrane Papers (Signed aboard HMS Orpheus off the Apalachicola River).

Capt. Hugh Pigot to Sgt. Samuel Smith & Corp. James Denny, May 21, 1814, Cochrane Papers (Signed aboard HMS Orpheus off the Apalachicola River).

Capt. William Rawlins to Admiral Percy Malcolm, February 26, 1815, Cochrane Papers (Sent from HMS Borer, "St. George's Sound").

Capt. George Woodbine to Capt. Hugh Pigot, May 25, 1814, Cochrane Papers (Edited and signed at Prospect Bluff on May 28, 1814).

Capt. George Woodbine, Talk to Council of Chiefs, May 28, 1814, Cochrane Papers (Given at Prospect Bluff).

Capt. George Woodbine to Lt. David Hope, HMS Shelburne, May 31, 1814, Cochrane Papers.

Capt. George Woodbine to Acting Lt. Samuel Smith, July 21, 1814, Cochrane Papers.

Capt. George Woodbine to Acting Lt. Samuel Smith, July 22, 1814, Cochrane Papers.

Capt. George Woodbine to Admiral Alexander Cochrane, July 25, 1814, Cochrane Papers.

Capt. George Woodbine to Admiral Alexander Cochrane, August 9, 1814, Cochrane Papers.

United States

Secretary of State John Quincy Adams to President James Monroe, September 19 1815, *British and Foreign State Papers, 1818-1819*, James Ridgway, London, 1835, p. 368.

Anonymous, extract of letter from Camp Jackson to Charleston, April 17, 1814, *New Jersey Journal*, May 31, 1814.

Anonymous, extract of a letter from a gentleman at Pensacola to his correspondent in New Orleans, July 25, 1814, *Louisiana Gazette*, August 16, 1814.

Anonymous, report from St. Mary's dated August 25, 1814, published in the *Georgia Journal*, September 7, 1814, p. 2.

Anonymous, Report from Milledgeville, Georgia, dated January 11, 1815, published in the *Baltimore Patriot* on January 30, 1815, p. 3.

Anonymous, Gentleman in St. Mary's to Gov. Peter Early, June 10, 1815, published in the *Georgia Journal* on June 21, 1815.

Anonymous, Gentleman in Fernandina to a friend in Savannah, June 10, 1815, published in the *Savannah Museum* on June 15, 1815.

Anonymous, Letter from Cartagena, August 25, 1833, published in the *Charleston Courier*, October 17, 1833, p.2.

Timothy Barnard to Mr. Munford, August 5, 1814, Hargrett Rare Book and Manuscript Library, The University of Georgia Libraries, Telamon Cuyler Collection, box 01, folder 11, document 15.

Timothy Barnard, Statement of "three confidential people" interviewed at Timothy Barnard's and interpreted by him, November 14, 1814, included in Hawkins to Early, November 15, 1814.

Abraham Bessent to Gov. Peter Early, August 20, 1814, Hargrett Rare Book and Manuscript Library, The University of Georgia Libraries, Telamon Cuyler Collection, Box 04, Document 04.

Brig. Gen. David Blackshear to Lt. Col. Allen Tooke, December 12, 1814, copy in author's collection.

Brig. Gen. David Blackshear to Col. Wimberly and Major Lawson, December 16, 1814, copy in author's collection.

Brig. Gen. David Blackshear to Gov. Peter Early, December 23, 1814, copy in author's collection.

Brig. Gen. David Blackshear to Gov. Peter Early, December 28, 1814, copy in author's collection.

Brig. Gen. David Blackshear to Maj. Gen. John McIntosh, December 30, 1814, copy in author's collection.

Brig. Gen. David Blackshear to Maj. Gen. John McIntosh, January 11, 1814, copy in author's collection.

Brig. Gen. David Blackshear to Maj. Gen. John McIntosh, January 14, 1815, copy in author's collection.

Captain Beekman of the merchant ship Hesper, Description of the death of George Woodbine, published in the *Alexandria Gazette*, September 5, 1833, p. 2.

Cappachimico (Kinhijee) to the Lower Creek Chiefs, undated, enclosed in Tustunnuggee Thlucco, Tustunnuggee Hopoi and John Stedham to Col. Benjamin Hawkins, June 13, 1814, Hargrett Rare Book and Manuscript Library, The University of Georgia Libraries, Telamon Cuyler, box 77, folder 33, document 23.

Chiefs to Col. Benjamin Hawkins, November 11, 1814, enclosed in Hawkins to Early, November 15, 1814.

Gov. Peter Early to Brig. Gen. David Blackshear, December 14 & 16, 1814, copies in author's collection.

Gov. Peter Early to Brig, Gen. David Backshear, January 6, 1815, copy in author's collection.

Gov. Peter Early to Brig. Gen. David Blackshear, January 10, 1815, copy in author's collection.

Gov. Peter Early to Brig. Gen. David Blackshear, January 16, 1815, copy in author's collection.

Gov. Peter Early to Brig. Gen. David Blackshear, January 19, 1815, copy in author's collection.

Benjamin Hawkins, "Report of supplies to the Indians by the British and Spaniards at Pensacola and mouth of Chattahochie," received by Governor Peter Early on June 17, 1814, published in the Georgia Journal, June 22, 1814.

Benjamin Hawkins to the Big Warrior, Little Prince and other chiefs, June 16, 1814, American State Papers: Indian Affairs, Volume I.

Col. Benjamin Hawkins to Gov. Peter Early, November 3, 1814, Hargrett Rare Book and Manuscript Libraries, The University of Georgia Libraries, Telamon Cuyler Collection, Box 76, Folder 25, Document 12.

Col. Benjamin Hawkins to Gov. Peter Early, November 5, 1814, Hargrett Rare Book and Manuscript Libraries, The University of Georgia Libraries, Telamon Cuyler Collection, Box 76, Folder 25, Document 14.

Col. Benjamin Hawkins, "Enrollment of Indians at their several dates up to the 14," Enclosed in Hawkins to Early, November 15, 1814.

Col. Benjamin Hawkins to Gov. Peter Early, November 15, 1814, Hargrett Rare Book and Manuscript Collection, Box 76, Folder 25, Document 28.

Col. Benjamin Hawkins to Jack Kennard, January 11, 1815, copy in author's collection.

Col. Benjamin Hawkins to chiefs of Am-mic-cul-le, January 11, 1815, copy in author's collection.

Col. Benjamin Hawkins to Gov. Peter Early, February 12, 1815, Hargrett Rare Book and Manuscript Library, The University of Georgia Libraries, Telamon Cuyler Collection, Box 76, Folder 25, Document 20.

Col. Benjamin Hawkins to Gov. Peter Early, February 12, 1815, quoted in Mark F. Boyd, "Historic Sites in and around the Jim Woodruff Reservoir Area, Florida-Georgia," River Basin Surveys Papers, No 13, *Bulletin 169*, Smithsonian Institution, Bureau of American Ethnology, 1958, p 270.

Col. Benjamin Hawkins to Gov. Peter Early, February 20, 1815, Hargrett Rare Book and Manuscript Library, The University of Georgia Libraries, Telamon Cuyler Collection, Box 77, Folder 25, Document 21.

Col. Benjamin Hawkins, Statement of U.S. Creek allies, quoted in postscript dated February 21, 1815, Col. Benjamin Hawkins to Gov. Peter Early, February 20, 1815.

Col. Benjamin Hawkins to Gov. Peter Early, February 20, 1815, quoted by Mark F. Boyd, "Historic Sites in and around the Jim Woodruff Reservoir Area, Florida-Georgia."

Col. Benjamin Hawkins to Gov. Peter Early, February 24, 1815, Hargrett Rare Book and Manuscript Library, The University of Georgia Libraries, Telamon Cuyler Collection, Box 76, Folder 25, Document 22.

Col. Benjamin Hawkins to Gov. Peter Early, February 26, 1815, Hargrett Rare Book and Manuscript Library, The University of Georgia Libraries, Telamon Cuyler Collection, Box 76, Folder 25, Document 23.

Col. Benjamin Hawkins to Gov. Peter Early, April 24, 1815, Hargrett Rare Book and Manuscript Library, The University of Georgia Libraries, Telamon Cuyler Collection, Box 76, Folder 25, Document 24.

Maj. William Lawrence to Maj. Gen. Andrew Jackson, September 15, 1814, republished in *The Cabinet*, October 26, 1814.

Little Prince, Talk at Coweta, November 1814, published in the *Georgia Journal*, November 23, 1814.

A. McDonald to Brig. Gen. David Blackshear, January 3, 1815, copy in author's collection.

Maj. Gen. John McIntosh to Gov. Peter Early, December 12, 1814, Hargrett Rare Book and Manuscript Library, The University of Georgia Libraries, Telamon Cuyler Collection, Box 47, Folder 04, Document 09.

Maj. Gen. John McIntosh to Brig. Gen. David Blackshear, December 19, 1814, copy in author's collection.

Maj. Gen. John McIntosh to Brig. Gen. David Blackshear, January 11, 1815, copy in author's collection.

Col. J.A. Pearson to Gov. William Hawkins, June 1, 12 and 13, 1814, *New Jersey Journal*, May 31, 1814.

W. & J. Pierce to Hon. Harry Toulmin, August 5, 1814, published in the *Western Monitor*, September 9, 1814.

Thomas A. Rogers, Letter dated at St. Stephens, Alabama, November 13, 1814, *Dedham Gazette*, December 23, 1814, p. 3.

Lt. Col. Allen Tooke to Gov. Peter Early, August 6, 1814, published in the *Georgia Journal*, August 10, 1814, p. 3.

Lt. Col. Peter Tooke to Gov. Peter Early, November 21, 1814, Hargrett Rare Book and Manuscript Library, The University of Georgia Libraries, Telamon Cuyler Collection, Box 47, Folder 04, Document 07.

Hon. Harry Toulman to Gov. Willie Blunt, August 14, 1814, published in the *Western Monitor*, September 9, 1814.

Tustunnuggee Thlucco, Tustunnuggee Hopoi and John Stedham to Col. Benjamin Hawkins, June 13, 1814, Hargrett Rare Book and Manuscript Library, The University of Georgia Libraries, Telamon Cuyler, box 77, folder 33, document 23.

Unidentified Red Stick chief to Col. Benjamin Hawkins, quoted in Hawkins to Gov. Peter Early, February 12, 1815,

Henry B. Wigginton to Col. Benjamin Hawkins, relaying the report of Capt. Timpoochee Barnard, December 2, 1814.

Spanish

John Forbes & Co. et. al. to Gov. Mateo Gonzales Manrique, March 1815, Cochrane Papers.

Gov. Sebastian Kindelan to Gov. Mateo Gonzales Manrique, quoted in Gov. Mateo Gonzales Manrique to Capt. R.C. Spencer, March 11, 1815, Cochrane Papers.

Gov. Mateo Gonzales Manrique to Capt. R.C. Spencer, March 11, 1815, Cochrane Papers.

Vicente Sebastian Pintado to Jose de Soto, April 29, 1815, Pintado Papers.

Newspapers

Alexandria Gazette
    September 5, 1833
Charleston Courier
    October 17, 1833
Connecticut Gazette

September 11, 1813
Louisiana Gazette
    August 16, 1814
Georgia Journal
    June 21, 1815
    August 10, 1814
    September 7, 1814
    November 23, 1814
    December 21, 1814
    June 21, 1815
London Times
    April 25, 1815
    August 13, 1818;
Savannah Republican
    December 22, 1815.
Lexington, Kentucky
    Reporter, May 10, 1815
Baltimore Patriot
    January 30, 1815.
Savannah Museum
    June 15, 1815
The Cabinet

    October 26, 1814
New Jersey Journal
    May 31, 1814.
Western Monitor
    September 9, 1814
Dedham Gazette
    December 23, 1814

Official Documents

American State Papers: Indian Affairs, Volume I, Gales and Seaton, Washington, D.C., 1832.

Cochrane Papers, Correspondence of Sir Alexander Forester Inglis Cochrane, Admiral, His Majesty's Royal Navy, 1814-1815, West Florida History Center and Archives, University of West Florida, Pensacola, Florida.

"Hawkins, Benjamin (1754-1816)", Biographical Directory of the United States Congress, http://bioguide.congress.gov

Pintado Papers, The Papers of Vicente Sebastian Pintado, Alcalde, commandant, and surveyor general of Spanish West Florida from 1799-1817, Special Collections Microfilm No. 900, West Florida History Center and Archives, University of West Florida, Pensacola, Florida.

Public Record Office, London, England, Colonial Office 23 and 24.

Registers of Enlistments in the United States Army, 1798-1914, Volume M-0, 1798-May 17, 1815, NARA M233, Roll Number 9, p. 179.

Treaty of Ghent, December 24, 1814.

Articles

Mark F. Boyd, "Historic Sites in and around the Jim Woodruff Reservoir Area, Florida-Georgia," River Basin Surveys Papers, No 13, *Bulletin 169*, Smithsonian Institution, Bureau of American Ethnology, 1958

Howarth, Stephen, "Cochrane, Sir Alexander Inglis (1758-1832), *Oxford Dictionary of National Biography*, Index Number 101005749, online edition, September 2011.

Sugden, John, "The Southern Indians in the War of 1812: The Closing Phase," *Florida Historical Quarterly*, Volume LX, Number 3, January 1982.

Books

Castelnau, Francis de Laporte, Comte de, *Vues et Souvenirs de L'Amerique du Nord*, Chez Arthus Bertrand, Paris, 1842.

Codrington, Sir Edward, *Memoir of the Life of Admiral Sir Edward Codrington*, 2 volumes, Edited by Lady Jane B. Bouchier, London, 1873.

Cox, Dale, *The Scott Massacre of 1817*, West Gadsden Historical Society/Old Kitchen Books, 2013.

Cox, Dale, *Milly Francis: The Life & Times of the Creek Pocahontas*, Old Kitchen Books, 2014.

Ridgway, James, *British and Foreign State Papers, 1818-1819*, London, 1835.

Saunt, Claudio, *A New Order of Things: Property, Power, and the Transformation of the Creek Indians, 1733-1816*, Cambridge University Press, New York.

Smith, Peter C., *Per Mare Per Terram: A History of the Royal Marines*, St Ives Press, 1974.

INDEX

Books by Dale Cox

Available in Print & Kindle editions.

Death at Dozier School
The real history of the controversial "Boot Hill" cemetery at the former Dozier School for Boys, a state reform school in Marianna, Florida.

Milly Francis: The Life & Times of the Creek Pocahontas
The remarkable story of an American Indian woman. She survived three wars and the Trail of Tears.

The Scott Massacre of 1817
The history of the first U.S. defeat of the Seminole Wars, a battle on the Apalachicola River that led to Florida becoming part of the United States.

The Claude Neal Lynching
The ground-breaking true account of the 1934 murders of Lola Cannady and Claude Neal in Northwest Florida.

The Battle of Marianna, Florida
A detailed history of the 1864 Civil War battle that culminated the deepest penetration of Florida by Union troops during the entire war.

The Battle of Natural Bridge, Florida
A history of the battle that saved Tallahassee from capture and preserved its status as the only Southern capital city east of the Mississippi not taken by Union forces during the Civil War.

The Battle of Massard Prairie, Arkansas
An account of the 1864 Confederate attacks on Fort Smith, Arkansas, this is the only book-length treatment of these little known actions that opened the door for the greatest supply seizure of the Civil War.

Old Parramore: The History of a Florida Ghost Town
A look back through time at the fascinating rise, life and disappearance of a riverboat town on the forgotten Florida section of the famed Chattahoochee River.

Two Egg, Florida: A Collection of Ghost Stories, Legends & Unusual Facts
The stories behind the stories of some of Northwest Florida's must unique legends, including the true history of the quaint little community of Two Egg.

The Early History of Gadsden County
A fascinating look at a series of key episodes from the pre-1865 history of Gadsden County, Florida.

The History of Jackson County, Florida: The Early Years
(Volume One)
A look at the pre-Civil War history of Jackson County, focusing on Spanish missions, Native American history, the Seminole Wars, the Antebellum era and more.

The History of Jackson County, Florida: The Civil War Years*
(Volume Two)
The most detailed account ever written of a Florida county's experience during the four years of the Civil War. Details battles, raids, outlaw gangs and more.
*Also subtitled *The War Between the States*.

A Christmas in Two Egg, Florida
A short novel or redemption set in the quaint Northwest Florida community of Two Egg.

All books by Dale Cox are available at:

www.exploresouthernhistory.com

www.ingramcontent.com/pod-product-compliance
Lightning Source LLC
Chambersburg PA
CBHW071054040426
42443CB00013B/3333